The Power of Love

A Guide to Consciousness and Change

Published in Great Britain 2004 by

MASTERWORKS INTERNATIONAL
27 Old Gloucester Street
London
WC1N 3XX
England

Tel: 0780 3173272
Email: books@masterworksinternational.com
Web: http://www.masterworksinternational.com

Cover artwork by Vanessa Kelly-Smith
General artwork by Vanessa Kelly-Smith and Liza Kay

ISBN: 0-9544450-4-X

Printed in the UK by Lightning Source

THE POWER OF LOVE
A GUIDE TO CONSCIOUSNESS AND CHANGE

by Phil Young and Morag Campbell

CONTENTS

Introduction	5
Chapter 1 Consciousness	9
Chapter 2 The Soul	27
Clearing the soul body gateways	34
Sensing your soul	36
Chapter 3 The Body	49
Clearing the physical body gateways	52
Physical body awareness exercise	56
Talking with your body-self	58
Enfolding your body in love	63
Walking in the presence of love	68
Chapter 4 The Mind	71
Clearing the mental body gateways	76
Chapter 5 Change	93
Freeze frame for change	102
Chapter 6 Relationships	113
Chapter 7 Sexuality	135
Pelvic release	144
Chapter 8 Love	153

INTRODUCTION

The basic essence of this book, its central theme if you like is that 'Love' is a tangible substance, the most important effect of which is to bring you in to a deeper understanding of yourself. This depth of understanding produces a change in your being, an expansion, which in turn facilitates the fullest possible expression of your unique potentials. Indeed, it could be said that the Power of Love will enable you to fully embrace all that is implied by the term 'Human Being.' To be fully human is a rare state for any man or woman to achieve. To do so requires an intimate, sustained and clear contact with one's soul on a daily basis. Your awareness of your soul or essence generates Love. Love brings light to the darkest recesses of your being and without that light there is no possibility of perceiving the oneness of all things. This book is entitled the Power of Love and we hope that by the time you have finished working with it you will have come to realise that there is a very real 'Power' in Love—a power for creating a new way of being for you in the world and in truth a new world for you to live in, a world embodying the power of Love.

If there is one place on Earth where the power of love is made manifest in the everyday beliefs and actions of its people, it is in the Pacific islands of Hawaii and through their philosophy generally known as huna. Although the word huna literally means 'that which is hidden' in truth the power of love is right there in front of us, so close that, like the air we breathe, we pay it no attention.

Generally when you hear of the Polynesian viewpoint on life called huna you often hear talk of the three selves. These are still further referred to as the Upper, Middle and Lower selves where the Upper self relates to the Higher conscious mind, the Middle self to the conscious mind and the Lower self to the unconscious mind. Whilst this is a common understanding of the Hawaiian perspective, it is, as you may have noticed, a model of Mind. In the true Hawaiian huna tradition it was never just a model of mind but rather of what is known as the three 'bodies' of man; the physical body; the mind body; and the soul body each with their own unique intelligence.

In the true traditional Hawaiian huna, physical, mental and spiritual wellbeing, was directly dependant on the level of communication between each of the three bodies. Awareness and integration of the three bodies was seen as crucial as was the acknowledgement of the constant presence of the ancestors, or personal Aumakuas, who watched over them, guided them and helped out when asked. This was at the heart of ancient Hawaiian life and led to a truly expanded state of being compared to the way in which Western man lives today. Ultimately, the goal of huna lay in the creation of a fourth body—an 'immortal spirit body.'

Our introduction to Hawaiian 'huna' was not the generally accepted route. We did not attend courses or read books on the subject. Indeed until a series of bizarre events began to unfold we had never even heard of 'huna' and our knowledge of Polynesian life was limited to the pictures of Gaugin and Elvis Presley's 'Blue Hawaii.' Our introduction to Huna can be described as nothing short of a major initiation.

When a powerful Kahuna, a priest magician, made a promise to his dying apprentice eleven hundred years ago on the island of Kauai, it seemed he needed someone in this time frame and life time to help him to fulfil that promise, and so we found ourselves drawn into a ancient world of divine practices and magic that was to change our lives forever.[1]

In order for him to keep his sacred promise, our personalities and belief systems; indeed everything that we held to be true about ourselves and our world, had to be cracked wide open to allow both these ancient beings to take over our lives.

At the end of this period we had both found a tremendous strength and belief in true love—love that has nothing to do with personality or projection but which is at the very heart of each of us. Love that is the essential part of all of us. Love which is a true reflection of the Divine. We had been exposed to the many possibilities of energy. Our minds had been stretched to encompass the impossible. In fact, if we could allow ourselves to get out of the way, the most amazing things could, and in fact, did occur. Things that often bordered on the miraculous.

It was also abundantly clear to us that throughout all of this we had been privy to the most amazing teaching. As much as this Kahuna wanted to fulfil his promise to his ancestors, he also wanted the ancient teaching, which was so much a part of him, to be shared. In this way he could once again find a state of balance, or 'pono' as it is called in Hawaii, after a vengeful act that he perpetrated all those years ago. This book is part

1. The detailed account of these miraculous events are told in 'A Promise Kept' by Morag Campbell also published by MasterWorks International.

of our work to share those precious teachings, known as Huna Mua, that we learned directly from Kiri and T'hane to give them their Hawaiian names. This book is a practical work book that explores in depth the nature of the body, mind and soul from the Huna Mua perspective and is a powerful tool for creating change in your life and giving love a real place in your world. To help you to achieve this, a number of practical exercises are included in each chapter. However, when you do these exercises be gentle with yourself, some of them need repeating more than once on a regular basis, but please do not get hooked in to an obsessive pattern of doing them. They should be done with clear intention, but always with a sense of fun and in the knowledge that you are perfect as you are, it is simply that it is always fascinating to explore new dimensions of awareness, new ways of being and to have more Love manifesting in your life. You may be wondering about the actual practical form these kind of changes might take. They may be as subtle as a shift in your perspective or as great as to totally transform the outer structure of your life, such as a new occupation, new relationships, or indeed a whole new life. Whatever manifests will reflect your soul's perception of the requirements that must be met for a life in which you can achieve full union between soul, body, and mind. It will be for the highest good of everyone concerned, although it may not seem so at the time. Later when you look back it will all be clear. Remember, understanding really only comes with hindsight.

When you read through this book it will seem as though it is saying that change, and an expanded state of being, is simple to achieve. We are sure that many of you believe this to be untrue. Yet we are all frequently given glimpses of ourselves as we could be, so called 'peak experiences,' times when we feel in tune with all that is, when we operate from a sense of 'knowingness' as opposed to just varying belief systems. The real difficulty lies in keeping in touch with this state throughout our daily lives. Establishing an unbreakable link with your higher self ensures constant access to this state of being. The reality is that having established this level of contact with your soul, growth and change are always a simple matter. The main requirement is that you maintain the link by keeping the gateways to your soul open. Never give up! The final outcome will more than justify any effort that you have to make. Your journey into the essence of who you really are begins here, now! Do you have the heart to turn the page?

Phil 'Kihonua' Young

Morag 'Kuoha' Campbell

CHAPTER 1

CONSCIOUSNESS

This book is an exploration of the universal phenomenon that is consciousness and in particular that quality of consciousness which is the tangible manifestation of Love. Before we look at consciousness in detail it is important for you to understand the particular perception of the nature of reality upon which everything in this book is based. This reality is that you are a multi-dimensional being living in a multi-dimensional universe. You exist in more than one dimension at the same time.

There are three fundamental dimensions or planes of existence within which human beings exist. They could even be referred to as individual universes. All dimensions or planes in a very fundamental sense are composed of space or the possibility of separation between the things which exist within that realm. The first plane is that of your soul, the 'universe of the soul.' It contains a huge variety of soul forms which are themselves formed of the basic element of that dimension which is life energy or life essence. The second is the plane of your physical body, the 'physical universe' which is filled with various organic and inorganic forms which are made from the basic physical elements within this dimension. The third is the plane of your mind, the 'mental universe' which has within it an enormous variety of thought forms which are made out of the basic element of this dimension, which we will call 'mind stuff.'

These three dimensions or universes fully interpenetrate each other so that the very centre of the physical universe is also the spatial location of the very centre of the mental universe and the very centre of the universe of the soul. Space in the physical universe is measurable in terms of feet and inches or metres and kilometres. In the soul and mental planes space behaves differently, in some sense it cannot be measured but separation between things still exists. Time also is not a fixed phenomenon in the three universes. In the physical and mental universes time is variable depending upon conditions and the relationship of events. In the universe of the soul however, there is no relational time flow, all things are happening at once or perhaps to be more accurate in no time at all.

Your own fundamental perception of reality is, in all probability, that you live in a very physical universe and that your mind, and perhaps your soul if you believe such exists, are part of that universe as well. To help you understand how you might confuse a multi-dimensional reality as being just a single plane of existence we suggest that you imagine each of these universes as being like a sheet of glass (figure 1). These three sheets of glass are exactly the same size and shape so that if you were to sandwich them together they would make what seemed like just one large complete piece of glass. Now if you were to take this image a step further by visualising that each sheet of glass had some writing on it, then when sandwiched together, all the writing would appear as if it were on just one single sheet of glass and make a single, consistent, meaningful statement. Yet in this analogy there are, in fact, three different sheets each with their own separate pieces of information or messages and in this example it is light that must pass through all three sheets for the information written on each to make sense. One of the of the basic reasons that life sometimes makes no sense is that for various reasons, staying with our analogy, light cannot pass through one or perhaps more of the sheets of glass perhaps because it is cloudy or misted over in some way and so the message is obscured and the meaning garbled.

In the case of the sheets of glass it is light that penetrates each sheet, or universe, and carries the information inscribed on each through to the other sheets and beyond. In the reality of the three universes it is '*consciousness,*' or perhaps more accurately the 'light of consciousness' that is the carrier beam which links the universe of the soul with the physical and mental universes. It is truly vital that the light of consciousness connect all three planes of existence for life itself to make any sense.

When awareness, which we will discuss in more detail shortly, operates in each universe or dimension, it generates a certain vibration or frequency of consciousness which carries information and experience from one plane to another. If you take just a few thoughts from this chapter let one of them be that 'consciousness is an information carrier.' To be able to carry information from one dimension to another consciousness must pass through gateways or warps in the fabric of the multi-dimensional reality in which you have your being. These gateways can become blocked allowing only a minimal flow of information between the three dimensions of existence. The laws which govern the light of consciousness are similar in many ways to the laws that govern the movement of light in the physical realm. This means that the light of

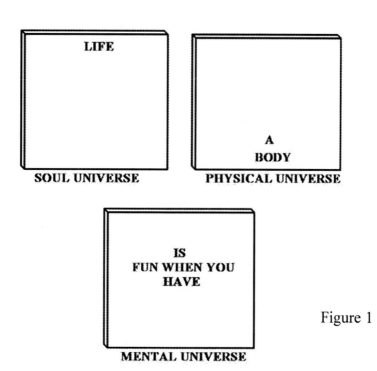

Figure 1

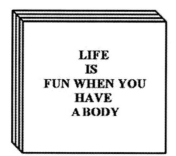

consciousness can be blocked, refracted, distorted or even extinguished, so it is possible for the intercommunication between the different dimensions of reality to be seriously disrupted. One of the purposes of this book is to familiarise you with all the dimensions and in particular the movement of consciousness between them. To bring light and clarity to your perception of reality.

At this point you may be wondering how consciousness is generated. Consciousness is a product of the action of Spirit. Specifically it is generated when awareness, which is itself an attribute of Spirit, is active. Spirit is a universal phenomenon. Pure Spirit exists throughout all dimensions in a quiescent state. It can not be located spatially as such because it does not show its existence unless it is active. When Spirit is active, awareness is functioning. When awareness is functioning, or we could say when Spirit is actively reflecting reality, then and only then is it possible to pinpoint its position in spatial terms. As soon as awareness ceases to function it is again impossible to tell its actual location. As awareness can manifest throughout the whole of your being we know that Spirit must be an all pervasive phenomenon but there isn't a separate Spirit for each dimension, it exists throughout all dimensions as a single unified phenomenon. Spirit is like a kind of backdrop to reality.

Truthfully, it is impossible to say in any ordinary human language exactly what Spirit is. That part of the universal, pure, undifferentiated Spirit that can manifest in the same spatial location as your body is commonly referred to in many Western religions and spiritual teachings as your soul. However, in our usage of language, the phenomenon of Spirit is something quite distinct from your soul. What you understand as 'being aware' is one of the functions of Spirit. Awareness is that which occurs when Spirit acts like a mirror that reflects experience or sensation derived from all the different kinds of activity that occur in each of the different dimensions of reality. Spirit also has the ability to self-reflect, in that it can within itself reflect secondary images of the primary reflections of the simple awareness of reality. Spirit reflecting or perceiving its own perceptions of experience is another experience in itself. In fact, when awareness functions in this self reflective way in the mental plane of existence it is the basis of what is commonly referred to as thinking. This self reflective capability of Spirit is the source of your 'self awareness.' In exploring the rest of the teaching in this book please do not confuse the word Spirit with soul. Spirit is a mirror that exists in each dimension, within each of your three bodies, and it is the source of your sense of self—your 'I'-ness. For much of the time Spirit is like a blank empty mirror. We can only know of its existence when it is reflecting something. The phenomenon of awareness then has two aspects, a passive receptive function, in which Spirit is acting as a simple mirror, and an active dynamic function in which it re-reflects or self reflects the original images again. In the passive function a single set of images is evident, in the active function this single set is reflected upon again and a complex image composed of multiple overlapping cross reflections is made manifest.

Since you are reading this book we assume that one of your main concerns in life is your own spiritual development. You may define this to mean that you are working to become more aware of your soul nature or something similar or to be able to live life in a more balanced and harmonious way. However, we would like to give you a rather different definition. Spiritual development is literally the development of a unique personal Immortal Spirit, what was referred to as an 'aumakua' in ancient Hawaii. It is actually possible to change the pure undifferentiated Spirit into a personal Spirit and because Spirit is indestructible it can become your own Immortal Spirit. It is possible to have a constant perception of the presence and location of Spirit by imprinting upon that pure Spirit an indelible image. When this happens Spirit is always reflecting something even if there are no reflections of current activity within reality. You could think of it as engraving or etching an image of your true self upon the pristine mirror of Spirit. The reflections in such a Spirit, and the consciousness generated when its awareness is active, is always subordinate to, and incorporates, the imprinted pattern.

To create a personal Spirit requires a complete integration between all the different dimensions of your being and congruent action in the outer worlds. In other words the creation and full expression of a true self. The creation of your personal Spirit is in reality not as difficult a matter as it sounds because you are all born with an innate integration between all the different dimensions of your being. The difficulties arise from the way in which you are raised to adulthood, a process that for many is fraught with problems. For some people due to fortuitous circumstance the creation of a personal Immortal Spirit is simple and easy. They never loose that innate integration that is the birthright of every human being, and, as they grow through life, they steadily imprint their true self upon Spirit. For those less fortunate much effort must be expended to re-integrate themselves, to be as little children once more. The information in this book is the key to regaining your birthright, your own immortality.

We suspect that you may be somewhat surprised, even stunned by the implications of the last paragraph, in as much as it is obviously saying that man is not inherently an immortal being. It is highly probable that you have always believed that your soul was immortal. It is a basic teaching of modern Christianity and indeed of many other religions. It is also a teaching espoused by the great majority of new age philosophies particularly those which are, in essence, based on the teachings of India or an esoteric form of Christianity. The understanding we are presenting to you is one that pre-dates most organised religions and is to be found mainly in the teachings that derive from primitive tribal beliefs concerning reality. It is, if you like, a more shamanistic understanding of reality. It is all too easy to dismiss the insights of older, supposedly less civilised cultures. The fact is, that so called primitive man, had in many ways a far superior contact with his soul and physical bodies than any citizen of the modern world. As an understanding of life it adds a very real urgency to your spiritual development. Create your own Immortal Spirit or perish utterly. There is a very real argument that the true underlying cause of the huge increase in the earth's population is occurring because fewer and fewer people are achieving immortality. The modern world is taking man further and further away from his true roots which lie in an understanding and experience of his own soul, body, mind and Spirit. Modern education is to a large extent totally inadequate to the task of educating human beings. Mind machines, yes—people, no.

In each of the different dimensions there exists for each of you a 'self,' or a complex pattern of self awareness. In the physical universe we will refer to this as your body self; in the mental universe as your ego or mind self; and in the universe of the soul as your higher self. What we would call your 'true character' is developed when your three selves are integrated into one unified or true self. For most of you what you refer to as your self or your character is probably a combination of your perception of your ego or mind self combined with perhaps a little colouration from either your body or soul. The function of awareness is, as we said, the basis of the sense of self in each of the different dimensions of your being.

Self reflection can occur within Spirit and be localised in only one dimension, or awareness can be active in at least two dimensions. Self reflection can occur between different areas of awareness within each body creating self reflective awareness that enhances the development of the 'self' within that realm. It can occur between two dimensions with the different qualities of consciousness being the 'light' that is reflected back and forth. Integration of your three selves to create a true self, to develop a character, requires that consciousness as a whole is exchanged freely back and forth throughout your whole being. This means that Spirit must be activated and awareness exercised throughout all the different dimensions of your being as often as possible. This will then generate consciousness in sufficient quantity so as to provide adequate light with which to see all the myriad reflections. For all this to be possible it is also vital that all the gateways between the different planes of your existence are clear.

No human being is ever fully aware all the time, nor is it a requirement that you should try to be. The continuity of your selves is facilitated beyond the activation of awareness by the function of memory. Each self still continues to function and exist even without your awareness being active, because in each dimension of your being there is memory. Memory that constantly supports the manifestation of the self. Memory which was created in any particular realm through the exercise of awareness. Memory itself is essentially the storage and maintenance of complex patterns of information over periods of time so that they can be accessed later. In the physical universe memory is stored in the cellular structure of your body in the form of complex chemical structures such as molecular bonds or patterns. These are stored throughout your body, not just in your brain. In the mental universe, memory is stored throughout your mental body in the form of complex patterns of mind stuff. Memory in the universe of the soul does not exist as such because it is a timeless domain and there is therefore a natural continuity and integrity in all the activity in the universe of the soul. Should you have developed a character, that too, is supported by memory in all three planes. It is important to know that the development of a character or true self carries with it no intimation that you will be fully aware all the time.

Once you have developed various patterns of response in relation to your awareness and perception of activity in any particular universe, and having reflected upon it, these patterns are stored as memories in either your physical or mental bodies, thereby creating a self. Then, even when you are without awareness, the perception of a pattern of activity in any realm will activate any corresponding pattern stored in memory which will then make you respond in a certain previously established way. When spirit is reflecting and self-reflecting the sensations related to your body in the physical universe then you are your body. When spirit is acting the same way in your mental universe then you will identify with your ego; 'I am my mind.' When you are deeply in touch with and aware of your deepest feelings then you are identifying with your higher self, or soul. Spirit is the common denominator. It pervades and acts in all three realms.

Due to the fact that your self is maintained by your memory we can say that your self is manifest even when you are not aware of it. The biggest problem with this is that your various selves are often outmoded by change and growth, in particular change within outer reality in the physical and mental planes. Your selves, and even your character, if you have one, should be consistently modified in relation to the continuing use of your awareness throughout your life. A true self is always a flexible phenomenon never a fixed state. This is why so called 'enlightenment,' must never be seen as some kind of ultimate state to achieve. It is a particular state of insight that is always relative to the changing conditions within reality. If you feel that you have achieved enlightenment that's fine but it is not an ending, a final resting place. In reality you must attain it again and again and again. Enlightenment is a dynamic process. You have it for an instant in relation to life as it is at a certain moment and then its gone. You are no longer enlightened until once again circumstances coalesce to create your enlightenment for just one more brief instant. We are always amused when we become aware of various esoteric and spiritual training courses promising instant enlightenment. Instant enlightenment is the only kind of enlightenment that there is! In each of the chapters that follow on soul, body and mind we will look in more detail at the selves relevant to each dimension and how to explore their nature as it already exists. Ultimately, the creation of a character, the formation of your true self will come with the application of all the insight and understanding that the exercises in this book offer.

All your experience and self reflections in any particular realm must be transferred to each of the other realms and be integrated into your experience in that particular dimension for there to be any kind of cohesiveness or congruence within your overall perception of who you are, the nature of reality and your relationship to it. Awareness in each of the dimensions of existence generates a quality of consciousness particular to that realm. Awareness of your life energy, which is synonymous with awareness of your true or pure feelings, generates soul consciousness or higher consciousness. Awareness of your thoughts generates mental consciousness. You may well identify mental consciousness with the whole of 'consciousness' when in fact it is only a part of it. This happens because most of you are more familiar with mental awareness and consciousness than any other. Finally, awareness of your physical body generates physical consciousness.

You have a physical body in the physical universe, a mental body in the mental universe and a soul body in the universe of the soul. The shape of your physical body, with which we are sure you are very familiar, is exactly mimicked by the shape of your mental body. Whereas the shape of your soul body is actually a large ovoid structure that is much larger than either of your other two bodies. The soul body forms after a spark of pure consciousness is thrown from the Divine. This Divine consciousness acts like a magnet and draws to it a great mass of life energy, a soul body. As spirit becomes active, the soul body becomes aware of itself. The soul consciousness generated flows in to the physical universe and begins the process of drawing two people together to create a new physical body that will be the vehicle through which the soul or higher self expresses itself in the physical realm. We say that the mental body mimics the physical body because the mental body comes into existence only after the creation of your physical body, and goes hand in hand with your physical development. Your mental body only begins to coalesce in the mental plane when the light of your physical consciousness begins to shine through the gateways between the physical and mental universes. This process only happens at a very low level whilst the foetus is still in the womb, but the greatest part of the development of the mental body happens after birth when the child's nervous system and brain begins to be bombarded by the incredible range of stimuli that the physical universe offers.

Once generated through your awareness, or the perception of events in any dimension, consciousness seeks to carry this information into the other planes of existence, to the other dimensions of your being. To do this it must be able to pass through the gateways or warps that exist between your various bodies to the other dimensions. Even though consciousness can be generated everywhere in your being there are also specific areas where it concentrates. Places where it gathers prior to its movement throughout the rest of your being and outer reality.

Physical consciousness concentrates in the brain and the location of the gateway through which it radiates into the mental realm is in the area of the medulla oblongata, an important physical structure at the base of your brain. It is vital that physical consciousness carries information through to your mental body. If this does not happen your mental body becomes an incomplete representation of your physical body and the mental consciousness that it in turn sends back into the physical body is flawed, which can create innumerable problems. There is another area in which physical consciousness also concentrates and this is in the area around your navel, the area of the so called abdominal brain, though in the modern western world it is an area of which most people have very little awareness. It too is the location of a gateway—a gateway into the universe of the soul.

Once the mental body has developed fully it has specific areas where mental consciousness gathers and gateways through which it travels into the physical realm. In most esoteric traditions these areas where mental consciousness concentrates are called 'energy centres' or 'chakras.' Their location in the mental body roughly equates with the location of the great nerve plexuses in your physical body. There are six of these centres and each could be considered as a small brain. They are places where a particular quality of mental consciousness will coalesce. Each chakra is also a gateway where the particular quality of mental consciousness gathered around it can shine through in to the physical plane. It should be clear from this that mental consciousness is composed of six different qualities or frequencies but all of these different qualities are but part of the whole, they must all be present in the appropriate amounts for the light of mental consciousness to communicate properly with the physical form. If this does not happen and only a certain part of the full spectrum of mental consciousness carries information concerning the mental universe to your physical body problems such as psychosomatic illness can develop.

When soul consciousness is created it tends to gather in that area of the of the soul body that equates to the chest area of the physical body. The light of higher consciousness also has to pass through gateways to get from the soul plane of existence to the physical plane. The gateways through which soul consciousness passes into the physical realm are at various points near the large spiral of life energy in the soul body that we call the soul pattern or seed pattern. Whilst soul consciousness passes through these gateways into the physical realm it does not have the ability to pass into the mental plane directly. Having reached the physical universe it must first be decoded by the body self, thereby becoming a part of the physical consciousness generated by it. Only then can the information that soul consciousness carries be passed on into the mental plane. This is why the sensation of life energy is always taken to be in the physical body by the mind when in point of fact it is actually in another dimension. The same is true of mental consciousness. It cannot pass directly in to the universe of the soul it has to first be decoded by the body self, become a part of physical consciousness, and then pass through in to the realm of the soul. In this sense the role of the physical body and the physical consciousness it generates is unique in that it can pass through into the mental universe and into the universe of the soul with equal facility. Thus the body and physical awareness is pivotal in terms of quality communication between all the dimensions of your being.

18

The actual impact of consciousness instantly affects the whole of each of your bodies but its decoding takes place predominately in certain areas. When considering the decoding and integration of consciousness it is important to remember that what we are exploring is the assimilation of the information that is carried by consciousness. In the physical body both the brain and the abdomen are places where the light of mental and soul consciousness is decoded, where all the information carried by these two qualities of consciousness is interpreted. The spinal area in your mental body is where the information carried by your physical consciousness is decoded. In the soul body physical consciousness is decoded throughout equally but there is a subtle concentration of activity in that part of the soul body that relates to the chest area. It is obvious that any blockage or disruption of the gateways between either the mental, physical or soul bodies is capable of causing a major severance between the different dimensions that go to make up a human being. We will be exploring, in greater detail, the various gateways through which consciousness passes in each of the following individual chapters on soul, body and mind.

All of the three qualities of consciousness generated, pass from one dimension to another, and have the information they carry assimilated into the awareness and experience of each universe. The feedback and exchange loops created by this phenomenon are incredibly complex and as we mentioned earlier any corruption of the free passage of consciousness through any gateway or its subsequent decoding can create major problems. Not alone does consciousness pass between the various realms of existence but it also carries information throughout the plane in which it was created. For example, mental consciousness carries information appertaining to activity within the mental universe and your mental body to the physical realm as well as distributing it within the mental universe. So, your mental body and your chakra system generate mental consciousness and interpret physical consciousness but they can also interpret information carried by mental consciousness emanating from other people. This accounts for one aspect of the phenomenon called telepathy. In fact, you are all telepathic and use the skill to a greater or lesser extent all the time.

At this point, having explored the generation, movement, and function of consciousness, we will now look in more detail at the nature and structure of consciousness itself. Unfortunately, we instantly run into a major barrier as there is no way in our language to describe the true nature of consciousness. However, all is not lost, as we said earlier the most appropriate phrase to describe what we are discussing is the *'light'* of consciousness. The actual properties of ordinary light in the physical universe go a long way towards illuminating the properties and structure of consciousness as a whole. The first thing to do is to look at light from a negative point of view—the actual absence of light. What is the experience in the physical universe of the non-existence of light? The answer, of course, is darkness—but what is darkness? What is left when the light is gone? The physical universe itself still exists but its quality is somehow profoundly different. How do you experience that possibility? What do you think about it? How do you sense it? What do you feel about it? To clarify your answers to these questions you might like to try the following visualisation.

Imagine that you are outside on a warm summer's night lying on top of a soft, grassy hill looking up at the stars. It is a beautiful, still, clear, moonless night. Experience this in as much detail as you can then allow yourself the perception that the stars, the points of light in the night sky are steadily disappearing until, within the space of a few minutes, you find yourself looking up into the night. A night where the atmosphere is crystal clear but where there is no star or moonshine. Allow yourself the fullest experience of that which is left—the dark. Store all your thoughts and feelings concerning the darkness so that you can remember them later.

This visualisation can be done either sitting or lying and, as in any visualisation technique, it is important to relax your body to some degree before beginning. It is always useful to focus on your breathing, making it deep, slow and easy as a way of relaxing your body. Always come back to normal awareness by stages and in your own time.

The thoughts and feeling you may have concerning the dark will be many but we suspect that, among your feelings, you might have experienced it as having a sense of quiescent power or perhaps a feeling of it being pregnant with possibility. Such feelings arise because by allowing yourself to fully experience the dark you are giving yourself an experience of the 'void' or 'Po' as the Polynesian's call it out of which all things manifest. You are in fact experiencing pure Spirit. Spirit before awareness is active, before consciousness is created. You are experiencing that place or space within which anything is possible. The womb of reality. Darkness is not really the absence of light, darkness is that which contains or absorbs all light. It is light in its unmanifest form. The actual absence of light is what you call 'shadow.' Shadow is where there is neither light nor dark. It is a place of distortion and silence. The dark void of Spirit is constantly resounding with the music of the spheres and the birth cry of new worlds.

Ordinary light in the physical universe has two aspects. It behaves both as radiant energy and as a particle with mass. Consciousness is also radiant energy and it too has mass. In what follows we will look at consciousness as radiant energy. We will consider its function as a particle, something with mass, in the chapter on change. As we pointed out earlier, consciousness of any particular quality, apart from carrying information through gateways to other realms of your being, radiates freely throughout the dimension in which it was created. For example, physical consciousness, generated in the physical realm carries information to both the universe of the soul and the mental universe. It also radiates throughout the physical universe. Here is where the analogy with light breaks down. It travels, not at the constant that is the speed of light in the physical universe, this being some 186,000 miles per second, but at any speed from perhaps only a few feet per second to perhaps many times the speed of light.

However, for consciousness to be able to radiate throughout any dimension it must be able to break free of what we will call the 'gravitational field of your being.' Even as a rocket must reach a great enough velocity for it to be able to break free of the earth's gravitational pull, so too must consciousness have sufficient energy to be able to break free of the gravitational pull of your being. This effect extends throughout each of the dimensions of your being. It is a critical factor in your ability to create the life that you want. Let us suppose, for instance, that you are a self employed business person and that you are working with a mental realm technique for bringing you more business by using an affirmation to the effect that your business is increasing greatly. If you cannot accelerate your mental consciousness to the velocity that is needed, so that it can break free of the gravitational field of your being, all that happens is that your affirmation and the consciousness it generates will come back to you. In other words, as you continue doing the affirmation you will become more and more acutely aware of how much you want your business to increase because your own consciousness, generated by the affirmation, is constantly there within the gravitational field of your being. This will in turn generate even more consciousness but still not necessarily of sufficient energy so as to be able to break free and move out into the mental universe where it can inform people of your need for them to use your business more often. An affirmation which does not energise your consciousness sufficiently just creates more and more congestion within your mental body until you give up the technique in disgust, probably thinking that affirmations don't work for you. An affirmation which does generate consciousness of sufficient energy to break free of your own field of being is literally a form of targeted cosmic advertising.

Most techniques for changing your world rely for their effectiveness upon your ability to be a radiant being. In our terms that is someone who radiates consciousness out beyond the gravitational field of their being with ease. A definition of a spiritual master is simply someone who radiates consciousness out beyond their being in huge quantities, all the time. It is not necessary for you to achieve this level of development so as to be able to change your world. Just a small amount of consciousness radiated out away from your being is often all that is required but to achieve even that takes a lot of skill and persistence. Skills which we are sharing with you throughout this book. You have to provide the persistence!

Before going any further, we will at this point, explore the nature of the different qualities of consciousness generated within the human being in more detail. If we look at the specific nature of each quality of consciousness generated in each dimension of your being as having the qualities of one of three great elements of the physical universe, we can go a long way towards giving you a qualitative understanding of them. The three great elements we are referring to are Fire, Water and Air. In this analogy the quality of soul consciousness is most appropriately described by the element of fire, physical consciousness by water and mental consciousness by air.

If we begin by looking at soul consciousness first, then to discover something of its true nature we can consider the qualities of 'fire' in the physical universe. When looking at physical fire we can say that it consumes things, it burns them and in that process transforms them into something different. During that process of transformation fire provides both heat and light. A flame always moves upward as it expands outward. It might also be interesting to consider all the different colours in which fire can manifest. All of these properties can, with a little imagination, be applied to the nature of soul consciousness. Soul consciousness therefore comes in many different frequencies or colours. It warms the soul body and provides illumination as well as having a transformative power. It is also the essence of the physical body's anti-gravity ability, something we will explore more deeply later on when we look at the physical body in detail.

When we look at the nature of water in the physical realm we see something which can, with some justification, be called a universal solvent. In its action as a solvent, water can change a substance from its solid form into a solution which is a combination of water and very small particles of the original substance to which the water was added. Thus we can also say that water exerts a transformative force. Water is also a lubricant. It allows things to move across each other without the creation of powerful frictional forces that might destroy them. Water always fills things from the bottom up due to the effect of gravity. Sometimes, this is expressed as 'water always seeks the lowest level.' When these properties are applied to physical consciousness it is possible to see that it provides a gently transformative dissolving force as well as being something which prevents too much friction. In terms of its actual effect on the physical body it both lubricates and nourishes it. It facilitates its change and growth.

When we look at the nature of air in the physical universe we can see that it moves incredibly freely and that it allows respiration and oxidation. It is intangible to your physical senses unless some force is acting strongly upon it making it move quickly. In the process of respiration oxygen is extracted from air so as to keep the living organism functioning and, in the process of oxidation, the oxygen in the air combines with another substance transforming it into something else. In the process of oxidation it also generates heat. In these two processes, air is both a transformative agent and yet is itself fundamentally altered at the same time. When filling an empty space it expands equally throughout. The effect of 'airy' mental consciousness on the mental body is that it always fills it up fully. The information it carries is also constantly combining and recombining with the basic element of the mental dimension creating new structures and providing a gentle warmth in the process.

In each case you can see that the three great elements each exert some kind of transformative action on the various substances in the physical universe. You can also see how each element has a nurturing effect upon all living organisms within the physical realm. By analogy we can see how vital the generation of each specific quality of consciousness is upon the three bodies that a human being is composed of. You can also see that each of your three bodies is transformed by the action of the consciousness generated within them. Consciousness as a whole is a transformative force as well as being essential to life itself.

Please do not take these analogies to the extent that you decide that there is an interaction between the different kinds of consciousness just because in the physical realm there are a number of reactions and interactions between Air, Fire and Water. The analogy holds true in so far as the effect of soul consciousness on the soul body and higher self is the same as the effect of fire in the physical realm. The effect of physical consciousness on the physical body and self is the same as the effect of water in the physical universe and the effect of mental consciousness on the mental body and ego is the same as the effect of air in the physical realm. However, there is no direct interaction between the three kinds of consciousness. Their only interaction is through the impact of the information that they carry on a particular body and its inclusion in the new awareness that is activated as a result. It should be obvious to you by now that the creation of consciousness in each of the different dimensions of your being, in each of your three bodies, is essential to the proper functioning of each body and the integrity and stability of each of your three selves.

Mankind is not the only being in reality who generates consciousness. All things within the physical universe have existence in the universe of the soul and in the mental universe also. Planet Earth, is a vast being with a soul body, a physical body and mental body. It has Spirit and so generates consciousness. It also has a sense of self, though different from that of a human being. It is through consciousness that you communicate with, and relate to, the Earth. Everything we have said previously in relation to the generation of consciousness and its function between human beings applies to the Earth and its family also. The Earth's family, its race or species if you will, are the other planets and moons in the solar system and any others that exist throughout the universe. The sun is of a different race or species than the Earth. Its family is the stars themselves.

Mankind, the planets, the sun, and everything else that is manifest, are interconnected by consciousness because all have some part of universal Spirit and all generate consciousness to a greater or lesser degree. Just as human consciousness is an information carrier within each dimension, and is also a link with the other dimensions of your being, so too does planetary consciousness carry information to other planetary beings as well as through to the different dimensions of its own being. It is possible for human beings to perceive and understand planetary consciousness just as they perceive and understand the consciousness of other human beings. The only problem with this phenomenon occurs for the most part when trying to interpret the patterns of information carried by planetary consciousness. The patterns held within the physical and mental consciousness are dependent upon the sense organs of the being that creates the patterns. The physical and mental sense organs of a human being are very different from the sense organs of a planetary being and so difficulties in interpretation are always a problem in the relationship between man and the Earth, when physical and mental consciousness is the language. However, soul consciousness, the consciousness developed by the soul body of a planet and also by the soul body of a human being are the same. The soul body of every being in existence is composed of the one life energy. This fact means that it is easy for you to interpret the soul consciousness of the planet just as the planet can easily interpret your human soul consciousness. Soul consciousness is a truly universal language. So now, having surveyed the reality of consciousness it is time to move on and look in detail at the nature of each of your three bodies in turn.

CHAPTER 2

THE SOUL

Your soul is the light within you. It is your intimate link with God and the rest of mankind. All the love you will ever need is already within you awaiting your 'self' realisation because your truest self, your higher self, is your soul. The soul consciousness which is manifested when you reside within an awareness of your feelings, your life energy, is 'LOVE.' To manifest your soul, to be your 'self,' is to be the truly human being that is your birthright. Your soul is the ultimate source of all your creative potential. Your soul is also perfect. Many spiritual teachings say that the soul incarnates on earth in order to learn and grow but in reality it has no lessons to learn. Its true challenge is to express itself as clearly and perfectly as possible throughout all the dimensions of reality. Your soul is full of good humour. It is here to have fun. You know you are in touch with your higher self when you feel a great and overwhelming joy, laughter and love of life bubbling up within you. Life, love and laughter are the foundation of your soul being.

Curiously, for many people the soul or higher self is little more than an idea or vague possibility that rarely impinges on the panorama of their thoughts. In truth in some cases it might be better to call the higher self 'the dweller in the dark' because some people have so little sense of its reality. It is as if your higher self is sitting in a darkened locked room somewhere in the 'house' that is your being, the key to which you lost long ago, a room whose exact location you have forgotten. Unless you have some degree of contact with or belief in the reality of the soul, your life is going to be little more than a random event in a meaningless universe. Your higher self can set up unique opportunities for the growth of your being but it can only do so with your awareness and with your willing participation. It can do all this because of its incredible ability to work with other souls and with the free unbound life energy that is the basic substance of the soul dimension of existence. Awareness of changes in the soul dimension and in your soul body, no matter how partial, can easily change the physical realm and your body through the enormous impact of soul consciousness generated. This is the power of love. This whole process is very dependent on the exchange of information between the three dimensions of your being. A belief in the reality of your own soul will go a long way towards keeping the gateways between it and the rest of your being clear. The kind of belief we are referring to is really not a belief at all but is more of a '**knowingness**.' A feeling that is much more potent than either opinion, faith, or hope. This feeling sense of '*I know,*' once acknowledged freely, can never be denied. You must know that your soul is real.

In simple terms, your soul body is composed of 'life energy' held within a certain form. Modern science has never been able to prove the existence of the soul nor the life energy of which it is composed but it is also true that science has no interest in proving the existence of such a concept or phenomenon because the whole idea of 'soul and life energy' cannot fit within any of the current major scientific paradigms. A scientist can only prove the existence of something and its properties if it is already within the structure of his mental processes, his world view. Nor will any scientist ever be able to prove the existence of this life energy until he can create a machine that can show something that exists in a different dimension to the dimension that the physical machine itself exists in! Unfortunately, this means that we cannot give your mind a nice rational scientific definition of life energy. It simply does not exist within those terms of reference. The meaning of that last sentence is very important because it does not say that life energy does not exist, just that it cannot be defined in our existing languages of mathematics, chemistry or physics. Curiously, everyone of you, scientists as well, have a machine that will register life energy already, the machine is *you*, a human being—hand built by God!

If we cannot define life energy in the kind of precise, rational, scientific terms that you are used to what then can we say about it? The most vital point about life energy is that your everyday perception of it is what your mind calls your 'feelings.' Not your emotions! Do not confuse feeling with emotion, they are quite different. Your perception of life energy is also synonymous with the sense of something moving in your body. It is what you experience in and around your physical body when you are powerfully stimulated, yet mentally still. It can be felt like tingling, fizzing, swirling, pulsating, vibrating sensations. It is fascinating to note that many of the ancient cultures that wrote of, or passed down oral traditions, concerning the life energy of the soul body, used terminology relating the experience of it in and around the body to the movement properties of water, air and light; the great natural phenomena that infuse the Earth.

To complicate matters, and this is very important, you must understand that what many cultures referred to as different frequencies or qualities of life energy are often in fact different frequencies of consciousness, carrying different qualities or kinds of information. At other times what they are referring to is more akin to what we would call the 'life breath.'

For the purpose of understanding the message of this book we would say that there is only one 'frequency' of life energy and this is the fundamental constituent of the soul body. In other words, in our terminology, 'life energy' refers specifically to that energy which is present in the soul body not to the more common definition of life energy which relates more often than not to the experience of the felt sense of inner movement which has specific links to the mind and breath. The more usual names for this inner activity are prana, chi or ki, these words come from the spiritual and medical teachings of various ancient cultures such as India, China and Japan. These terms which are usually translated into English as simply 'life energy' or 'breath energy' are ubiquitous and were used throughout different periods in the history of these cultures to refer to phenomena connected variously with not just soul but with thought, breath and vitality. Influencing the activity of these energies formed the basis of much of the healing work done in these cultures. This kind of life breath energy is what we refer to as the activity within the mental body. It too flows, pulsates and vibrates but it is a coarser phenomenon than, in our terminology, the 'life energy' or the 'feelings' in the soul body.

So to reiterate, what we are saying is, that many of the different approaches to healing that you may have experienced or read about use the term life energy to describe the processes they are interacting with, whereas to be more specific, we would rather say that what these practices are working with are the manifestations of the life breath, the primary basis for which is predominately the activity in the mental body. Later on when we are exploring the mind we will examine this 'life breath' in more detail.

Your soul body is, as we said, composed entirely of life energy. Its shape is not that of the human body but is a tear-drop shaped structure (Fig 2 and 2a). The predominate pattern of flow throughout this structure is an overall expansion and contraction and within this overall movement individual particles of life energy move in small tight spiralling arcs. The soul dimension is itself full of free moving life energy. This energy is formed into a soul body when a spark of Divine consciousness emerges into the soul dimension. So, whilst in the previous chapter we said that a human being had three

Figure 2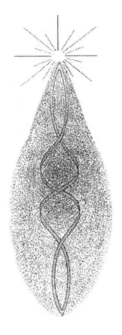

Figure 2a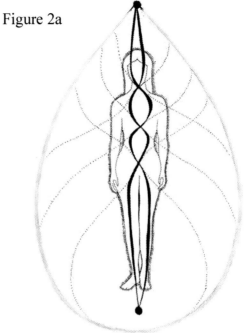

Figure 3

Figure 4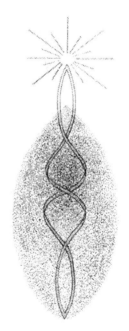

dimensions, absolute reality is in fact composed of at least four plus 'Spirit,' though we can not talk to you of this fourth dimension. This is the realm of the Absolute, or God in which divine consciousness has its origin and cannot be described in any human language. It is simply the Source of All Things. In the domain of the soul and of the life energy it is the emergence of a spark of Divine consciousness that is the force behind the creation of the soul body. When a spark of Divine consciousness emerges into the realm of life energy it attracts to itself a concentration of the basic element of that dimension and creates a binding pattern or an organising matrix for it. It is this pattern which creates and maintains the structure of the soul body. This binding pattern is the embodiment or carrier of the information contained within Divine consciousness. It is an intensely concentrated pattern of life energy whose basic shape is that of a large double spiral or double helix (fig 3). This pattern, which is the binding or organising pattern in the realm of the soul, is similar to the binding pattern in the physical realm which is the DNA molecule. Both have a similar shape, each being two intertwined spirals. There is an innate resonance and relationship between the binding pattern created by Divine consciousness in the universe of the soul and the DNA molecule. DNA is the organising matrix in the physical universe, which is itself created by soul consciousness as it emerges into the physical realm. Each fulfils exactly the same purpose and has the same overall pattern.

The soul pattern, which carries the information brought in to the soul plane of existence, exerts a powerful attractive influence upon the free life energy and forms it into the tear-drop shaped soul body. The soul pattern is first created by the appearance of Divine consciousness in the universe of the soul. The form of the soul pattern is fixed and does not change throughout life. However, the shape of the soul body that it wraps around itself can change. In some cases the upper part of the soul body, near the location of the gateway through which Divine consciousness emerges, can become weakened or distorted in which case the soul body becomes more egg shaped (fig 4). That is a soul body whose free moving life energy, or to use the Hawaiian term 'mana,' no longer comes into direct contact with Divine consciousness. A soul being whose link with its source is subtly corrupted. At physical birth and for some time thereafter, usually up to the age of two, the link between the soul body and Divine consciousness is extremely strong and clear. However, as the mental body gains in strength and as the child becomes 'educated' the link tends to become less active and, indeed, in extreme cases the feeling of being in touch with Divine consciousness is lost. In this case the person has become what you could call a 'lost soul.' A soul whose feeling link with Divine consciousness is no longer active. The whole being of a person in this state is affected should this situation arise. In the physical realm it is often characterised by pain and organ malfunction, whilst in the mental realm it is frequently accompanied by a profound loss of heart, a loss of the sense of the meaning of life. It is possible to heal this kind of damage. In fact, in a sense this whole book is about the resolution of this problem. However, the bound life energy within the soul pattern itself always touches the transpersonal gateway and is therefore in constant touch with Divine consciousness. The only time that particular link is broken is at the dissolution or death of the soul body. One of the most important things to remember is that at the deepest core of your soul body, through the soul pattern, you are always in touch with Divine consciousness.

The soul plane of existence, the realm of life energy is a timeless zone where the free unbound energy that exists within it is in a constant spiralling movement. However, when a large amount of life energy is created, as in a soul body, the life energy begins to pulsate through the attractive effect that individual particles of life energy exert on each other, an effect that is greatly intensified when in concentration. In reality the creation of the spiralling soul pattern and the soul body is instantaneous, or to be more accurate, it takes place outside of time or indeed in no time at all! The impact of Divine consciousness on the soul pattern is so great that the pulsation that would normally occur within it is inhibited. This phenomenon gives rise to what we will call the fundamental nature of the soul. This is determined by the phase of movement within the expansion-contraction cycle of the life energy within the soul pattern. If the bound life energy in the soul pattern is held within the expansion phase then we would say such a soul was a Light Soul. If the life energy in the soul pattern was in its contraction phase of movement then the soul is called a Dark Soul. Please try and read these two terms without them having any connotations of good and bad for you. It is simply a convenient form of differential labelling not a value judgement. We could just as easily called them blue souls and red souls. It is important to realise that there is no advantage to having a soul pattern whose nature is expansive rather than contractive, light rather than dark, and vice versa.

The structure of the soul body is maintained by Divine consciousness and the spiral binding pattern that it creates; the soul pattern. The location at which the spark of Divine consciousness emerges into the realm of the soul is always just above the top of the tear drop of life energy that is the soul body. This place is the gateway through which Divine consciousness passes into the universe of the soul and it is also through this same gateway that soul consciousness passes back into that unknown fourth realm of existence. We call this gateway the Transpersonal gateway or Stargate. In the physical realm it is located approximately eighteen inches above the top of the head. The physical location of the gateways through which soul consciousness passes in to the physical realm are in the location of the throat, both shoulders, both breasts, over the liver and spleen, and in the region of the pubic bone (Figure 5). These gateways penetrate through the body and are located on both front and back. For those of you who always like to know the reason why things are the way they are, there is unfortunately no rational explanation as to why these gateways occur in the pattern that

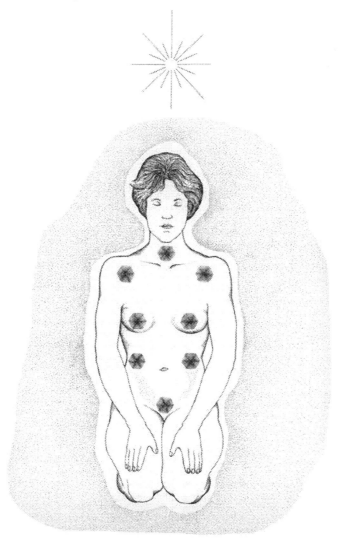

Figure 5

33

they do. That is just the way that reality designed it, though of course some of you interested in comparative studies of esoteric philosophy might like to speculate on its similarity to the structure of the kabbalah.

CLEARING THE SOUL BODY GATEWAYS

To facilitate the passage of soul consciousness through the gateways into the physical realm you can use one of the following techniques. Before you begin, study figure 5 carefully so that you are fully aware of the location of the gateways. The first method can be done either sitting or lying in a comfortable position and is fundamentally a visualisation technique.

To begin, construct somewhere in the internal space of your mind an image of a hollow tube about 10 inches or 25 centimetres long with a diameter of about 1 inch or 2.5 centimetres. See if you can create it out of some thin translucent glassy substance. Once you have created a tube move it down to float in front of your pelvis with one of the open ends pointing towards you. Now move it towards the place where you sense your lowest soul body gateway to be located, usually this will be just above your pubic bone. Allow the end to lightly touch that area of your body. Now, very slowly allow it to penetrate into your body, feeling any internal sensations as you do so until it is completely inside you. Repeat this same process, using a new tube each time, on all of the other gateways working upwards. Allow yourself a few moments to experience any other internal feelings for each of the other gateways, finishing with the gateway that is located in the throat area. Depending on your actual physical size some of you will find that the ends of the tube protrude both front and back and others will find both ends of the tube are inside the body. Having completed this action create another tube and repeat the same process

For the sake of completeness you may include the transpersonal gateway in this exercise if you wish, but it is not essential as it is not a gateway through which soul consciousness emerges into the physical realm which is the focus of this exercise. If you have difficulty with visualisation exercises it is possible to get someone else to do a soul body gateway clearance on you as a kind of hands on bodywork technique.

To do this, lie down on the floor or on a massage table and your partner, who is doing the clearance, will stand or kneel on your right side and then place their right hand palm down on your pelvic gateway (just above the pubic bone) and their left hand palm down over the liver gateway (just over the floating ribs on the right side of your body). Then, and this is an important part of the technique, they must imagine that their hands are becoming insubstantial in some way by perhaps imagining them as turning into silver light or liquid light. Then, once this alteration to the sense of their hands is clear they should have the feeling that their hands are slowly sinking or penetrating down through your physical body deeper and deeper thereby activating a tunnel of spirit or awareness until they come to a depth at which they feel comfortable, where they can happily rest their awareness of their hands and then do absolutely nothing! If they allow themself the understanding that there is an infinite amount of space inside your body then they won't feel as though their hands have popped out of the back of your body but they will perceive them as still being inside you throughout the process. They must just allow themself to be there within you, not trying to do anything, just being there for a minute or two and then they can withdraw their awareness and repeat the same process with each of the following sets of connections moving the hands to each of the following positions; liver gateway and right breast gateway, right breast gateway and right shoulder gateway, right shoulder gateway and throat gateway, throat gateway and left shoulder gateway, left shoulder gateway and left breast gateway, left breast gateway and spleen gateway, spleen gateway (just over the floating ribs on the left side of your body) and pelvic gateway. Finally, making three connections across the body firstly spleen gateway and liver gateway, left and right breast gateways and then both shoulders to finish. Throughout this exercise you simply lie passively, as relaxed as possible, feeling anything that might be happening internally.

When actively doing this technique your partner should, for comforts sake, move to stand by your left side when making the connections on that side of your body. It is not important that they understand the purpose of the exercise for the technique to be effective, just that they can visualise their hands sinking down inside your body. It is also perfectly reasonable for you to offer to do the same clearance on them. The act of 'not doing' when performing a gateway clearance on someone is of the utmost importance. We are all addicted to doing things but this technique needs you to simply 'be,' The only 'doing' in this exercise is the visualisation of the hands becoming insubstantial and then sinking inside your partner's body. There is nothing specific that you should or should not feel when either giving or receiving a gateway clearance, just be there with whatever is happening. After clearing your gateways it is much easier to be aware of the reality of the life energy that is your soul body.

SENSING YOUR SOUL

To actually explore your soul body itself you can begin by standing up and stretching your arms straight up above your head. Then allow your arms to fall downwards and outwards sideways away from each other keeping the arms straight until they are at shoulder height. In this movement you have touched the extremities of your soul body in a side cross section. Now stretch your arms out straight in front of you at shoulder height and lift them slowly straight upwards. The arc of movement here describes the forward part of the upper section of your soul body. If you could imagine doing this same movement but with the arms directly behind you it would delineate the boundary of the upper rear portion of your soul body. Do you begin to see with the help of these movements and a study of figure 2a the full extent of the three dimensional form that is your soul body? It would be useful to reflect for a few moments on the sheer size of this your soul body, a part of you so big and yet of which you have so little awareness.

Another simple movement which we like to call 'embracing the soul body' is simple and easy to do as well as having some excellent general benefits. Stand with your feet about shoulder width apart with the feet parallel. Stretch your arms up above your head, keep them straight but this time with the backs of your hands just touching so that the palms face outwards. Now drop both arms sideways, down and outwards, at the point at which your arms reach just below shoulder height begin to bend your knees dropping steadily into a squatting posture as your arms continue downwards. Let your body incline forwards as you bend down. Allow your arms to draw inwards and together as you nearly touch the floor with your fingertips. The whole movement is a large scooping gesture that describes a cross section of your soul body. Let your palms meet together at the bottom of the movement and then bring them up the centre line of your body with the backs of the palms partially turned towards each other. At this stage your elbows are bent. Continue the movement until your arms are stretched upwards above your head, the palms rotating until they face outwards once more and at this point you can continue with the complete cycle all over again. Do this for about a minute or so keeping your physical body relaxed, moving easily and fluidly. Once you have done the movement rest with your arms relaxed by your side and allow yourself

36

to be aware of the space that surrounds you. Experiment with doing the movement at different speeds from slow to fast. However, do not allow yourself to do the movement in such a way that you become breathless or tired as this will block your awareness in the final sensing stage.

Your soul body is your feeling body. It should not be confused with what is referred to in some spiritual teachings as the astral or emotional body. That particular phenomena is an aspect of your mind and mental body. Your soul is the source of your true feelings and these feelings have a unique constancy throughout your life. Your feelings are 'the still, small, quiet voice within,' the voice of your soul. This soul language is not a verbal one. We are not speaking of a language like Russian, English or even Chinese but a universal form of communication common to all people regardless of race or creed. What you experience in those few odd moments in life when you exclaim, at the very least inwardly, 'I feel so alive,' is no less than an experience of your own soul. It is an awareness of the movement of the life energy within your soul body, a 'feeling,' which generates soul consciousness. A quality of consciousness whose fiery impact upon your soul and physical bodies is so great as to tear such an exclamation from the heart of your being

For a moment just allow yourself the luxury of sitting somewhere in a very comfortable position and see if you can recall such a moment of aliveness in your own life. Remember it in as much detail as you can. What caused it, what was happening in the world around you, was anyone with you? Having recreated the whole scene in your mind's eye go inside and ask yourself what you 'feel' now, at this very moment, as you recall the experience. What are you aware of feeling in and around your physical body. What do you feel? Are you aware of any fizzing sensations? Are you warm? Where do you feel movement? What shape is it?

Please be aware that the sensations or feelings that we are talking about are very subtle. It is important to look beyond and beneath the gross intense sensations that have more to do with emotion than feeling, mind than soul. You can do this exercise in relation to any aspect of your life. Try evoking within yourself the daily work that you do, then see if you can discover what your soul feels about it. The answer may surprise you. What might it mean if you could feel nothing or perhaps just some sense of contraction or stillness? It could well be that your soul's needs are not served by your work in any way. We suggest that you explore the whole of your life in this way to discover how your soul feels about it. This exercise will be an in depth exploration of your own higher self and how it feels about your life. If you feel nothing at all in any

37

of these experiments it is simply that in all probability you are not yet quite tuned into the subtle quality of experience that is soul feeling. Just persevere with the exercise over a period of time and we are certain that you will find a whole new world of experience opening up. It is the subtle almost ethereal nature of the experience that initially causes some difficulty, but it does pass.

Many modern authors have gone to great pains to point out the growing similarity between the language of current thinking in the area of quantum physics and that of the mystics' concept of the nature of the world. Whilst these books are fascinating reading, until the being of the quantum physicist actually and totally embraces the dimension of the soul, the parallels with the mystics' understanding of life, which is itself based on intimate contact with the soul plane of existence, are only of curiosity value. Such books have no impact on scientists' mechanistic view of the world, the roots of which lie much deeper. So these scientists still go on creating more and more powerful weapons based on their knowledge, more global pollution through new industrial processes and even the possibility of perverting the whole nature of human life at the physical genetic level is now a reality.

The real problem lies in the scientist's lack of contact with their soul, the source of their true feelings. Indeed it is unfair to just single out scientists as this problem is also true of the great majority of the rest of mankind also. In essence, there is a fundamental lack of integration between the body, soul, and mind within most people. When, and if, science accepts the reality of the soul and that the quality of integration between all the different dimensions of the being of any scientific researcher is of absolute and paramount importance, then, and only then, will a truly humanist science evolve. If this happens science will finally be of real benefit to us all. In the final analysis, what science lacks is understanding and knowledge that is infused with real feelings. As it now stands most modern science is lifeless theory, without heart and soul.

At this point it is important to state again that the life energy does not exist in the same dimension as the physical matter within the universe. When you hear people say that energy flows in the body, regardless of what kind of energy they are referring to, be it the one life energy or mind energy and whether they realise it or not, they do not mean that it flows in the body in the way that blood flows in the body. Blood is a physical substance that moves through the structure of the physical body, whereas life energy is a non-physical substance that exists in a different dimension to the physical structure of the body. The fact that life energy does not exist in the same dimension of space and time as physical matter is, as we said, the major reason why science has not discovered this life force. The confusion arises because the different dimensions of existence are superimposed upon each other, but are, if you like, out of phase. It is quite possible to confuse the location and nature of the awareness of activity within any of the three bodies.

The interface between the world of the soul, the realm of life energy, and that of physical matter, is the particular quality of consciousness that we refer to as soul consciousness. Remember, consciousness has the ability to cross the barriers between the dimensions by virtue of it being of a different fundamental nature than the basic structure of any dimension. To be precise the link between the realm of the soul and the physical realm is the 'light of soul consciousness.' In the physical world, science has long known that light has the ability to behave both as a particle of matter or as a wave of pure energy. You may also be aware that many people who are able to perceive the subtle realms of existence see them as a brightness, or radiance around a person. In fact, it is often the case that what they are actually tuning into is a visual perception of the movement of consciousness itself not the shape of the one body of life energy that is the soul body. These qualities of 'radiance and brightness' are in themselves descriptions of certain properties of light and if you remember we have already given the analogy of soul consciousness in particular as being like fire. Fire, of course, is a source of light. The relationship between consciousness and light is also shown to some degree in everyday speech when a particular person is described as being totally 'radiant' for example. Soul consciousness is the carrier beam of the information that flows from the realm of the life energy to the physical universe. It allows activity in the universe of the soul, in the first instance, to create and, later to continue to, influence the physical body.

Your awareness of any changes in the activity or feeling in your soul body has an instant impact upon your physical body. However, because one of the major differences between the physical dimension and that of the soul is a difference in time flow if we may call it that, the speed at which events are perceived to occur, it is not possible to predict how long changes in the activity in the soul body that are carried by soul consciousness to the physical realm will take to manifest as changes in the physical world. In the realm of life energy relational time does not exist. In the physical dimension time flow is not uniform and can vary anywhere from very slow to extremely fast. It is therefore possible for any kind of change in the activity in the soul dimension of existence to have a virtually instantaneous effect on the physical world or sometimes for that physical change to take days or weeks to occur. However, changes in the physical dimension of being, the information concerning which is carried by physical consciousness back to the realm of life energy always creates changes in the flow of life energy instantaneously. The reason we have called this to your attention is that any and all of the practical exercises in this chapter can have an enormous effect upon the functioning of your physical body. Effects that may occur almost instantly or take a few weeks to manifest. Either way they will always constitute a profound healing if that is what is required. Though, of course, if your physical body is healthy no changes are likely to occur, though you might find that your mind has changed in some way instead.

In our terms spiritual development is literally the development or creation of an Immortal Spirit. In the previous chapter we spoke of the imprinting of universal Spirit, its 'personalisation.' The creation of an Immortal Spirit self is achieved by generating consciousness in all three dimensions of your being, ensuring that it flows freely between each dimension, and by integrating the information carried by it into the fundamental nature of each of your three selves. In the first instance, this leads to the creation of a fully congruent sense of self in all dimensions and ultimately over a period of time, as you live fully from this integrated self, the universal Spirit that is part of your being becomes imprinted with the essence of this integrated self thereby finally creating your Immortal Spirit self. The imprinting of universal Spirit occurs through the enormous impact of the conscious generated by someone with an integrated self in three dimensions. This integration can only happen when consciousness can pass freely from the realm of the soul through to the physical realm and then on to the mental realm and back again along the same pathway. This imprinting is the patterning of Spirit with images of your integrated self. After this stage any time Spirit is active anything that is reflected in it is superimposed upon the indelible images of your self that are already held there. All your self reflections in Spirit are thereby related to, or referenced to, your Immortal Spirit self. In essence this means that all your actions, thoughts and feelings stem from a totally congruent source, a fully integrated sense of self.

There are many spiritual traditions that use a hierarchical model of creation in which God is seen to create the soul, the soul gives rise to the mind, and the mind the physical body. Spiritual growth or evolution is often characterised in these traditions as a 'return to the source.' What is meant by this is that the soul is said to have descended from Spirit or God to involve itself into the world of matter in the form of the physical body. At this point its need is to transform itself and evolve back to Spirit.

This commonly held concept of spiritual evolution nearly always seems to be misunderstood. The process of Spirit becoming matter or involution is in most of these teachings seen as a fall from grace. The soul is believed to have lost something of inestimable value during the process of involution. The physical body is seen to be a snare which the soul has become caught up in and is therefore a serious impediment to spiritual evolution. This understanding leads the people who follow such teachings to pursue what we might call the springboard concept of spiritual growth. What we mean by this is, that to evolve spiritually they literally reject the reality of their physical body as a trap that is capturing them with its needs and desires and presumed lack of divinity due to its distance from the source. They then try and use this belief as a springboard to jump off from so that they can return to Spirit. It is as if their mind is constantly trying to jump out of the body to get back to God. They assume that their rejection of the body will be viewed, at a soul level or by their own conception of God, as their most vital act, in the pursuit of their spiritual evolution, for which they will be justly rewarded.

Much of the confusion arises because many of the teachings say that the soul is immortal and that since the body is not, it can, and indeed should be, disregarded as unreal when pursuing the path of spiritual development. It is also taught that the mind can somehow be elevated or spiritualised by constantly focusing it on God, the soul and spiritual development. In reality spiritual evolution is only possible because you have a body. The rejection of the physical form inherent in these teachings is wrong. The body is not something to be escaped from it is something which you must go through and experience fully and totally. In simple terms this concept of evolution is going against the natural flow of consciousness.

Divine consciousness creates the soul, soul consciousness creates the physical form and physical consciousness creates the mental body. Consciousness then begins its return flow from the mind through the body back to the soul and finally returns to its divine source. Spiritual growth is, above all, an entirely natural process. Nor is this understanding that we are sharing with you hierarchical in any way. All aspects of your being must be developed and function together in harmony. No one aspect is paramount. There is no way that going against the flow, by rejecting the fundamental divinity of the physical form that is the human body, and mistakenly elevating the mind to a position where it is seen to create and sustain the body, can lead to anything other than a false experience of 'spiritual' growth. To deny the body is to break the flow and transformation of consciousness that is essential to spiritual development. The body is the critical link between the soul and mind. The soul and the body are fundamentally linked through the creation process. To reject the body is to reject the soul. Furthermore, neither the soul, the body or the mind are immortal. Immortality can only be achieved through the creation of an Immortal Spirit Body. Please be very clear about this issue and indeed we suggest that you read these last two paragraphs again and don't think about what we have said but feel about it. Look for your soul response.

As you become better able to express your true soul nature so you become able to aid it in the creation of an Immortal Spirit. In expressing your soul, you give it the opportunity to send its consciousness, its love out into the world as well as through your own being to do work. It is received by the world and creates transformation before being returned to its source. The more freely you radiate love and accept all that returns to you, the greater is the degree of transformation within your being and the greater the possibility of creating an immortal self. There is an imprinting that occurs as the transformed consciousness returns to its source, your soul or higher self. You, through your embodiment in the physical and mental worlds, are the medium through which the soul expresses itself and also the vehicle that gathers the consciousness as it returns. As the consciousness returns some of the essential nature of each of your other two selves becomes part of your higher self and the soul consciousness generated by your awareness of this unique composite self will over time imprint its personal nature on the pure undifferentiated Spirit that is part of you. Your ability to generate and express your soul consciousness is the key to the creation of your own Immortal Spirit.

One of the most frequently discussed aspects of the soul and spiritual growth is the concept of Karma. Karma, in the usual sense of the word, is the law of cause and effect. Every cause must have an effect and every effect in itself can become another cause. In an everyday context the meaning of karma is often taken to be that if you act in a way that causes someone else pain or suffering then there is a universal law that requires that you experience someone causing you the same pain or suffering as a balance. Indeed Karma is often seen to be an inescapable law of earthly existence. The need for this law to be satisfied will often transcend time and space thereby causing a person to incarnate into a physical body again and again over a period of many centuries, through many lifetimes. The truth is that for most people Karma in this sense simply does not exist. There are multitudes of people creating intense suffering in the world due to their personal greed and avarice. This suffering is not being balanced because the law of 'cause and effect' has no impact upon a human being who has lost touch with their soul. They can be totally amoral and experience no 'effects' in relation to the causes that they introduce into the world except that gratuitous satisfaction of their own desires at the expense of others. It is only when you have soul contact that you know the effects of your actions upon other people and the Earth itself. It is only with soul contact that you acquire a conscience. Conscience is the force behind the law of Karma. If you want to transcend the Law of Karma then avoid pursuing any form of spiritual development! If you accept the fact that man is not automatically immortal then you can see that should a person act in life without conscience, when they die they perish forever, nothing survives. Actually, this could be said to be the lawful or Karmic result of their actions, to be totally annihilated! We would also point out that if you have soul awareness, and thereby a conscience, then cause and effect can become an almost instantaneous phenomenon. Accelerated, or instant Karma as it is often called, is the only kind of Karma that exists for people with a good soul connection. It does not need to function over many lives as generally it is far more powerful than that though in some circumstances it has to work over a number of lifetimes to be fully resolved.

If someone has developed an Immortal Spirit Body, no matter how vestigial, they do not have to reincarnate so as to balance out the effects of any of their previous actions in earlier lives, but simply to have the opportunity to perfect their spirit body. It is this growth process that gives rise to the phenomena of reincarnation, not the needs of the Law of Karma. If you have managed during your life on Earth to create an Immortal Spirit Body but have not perfected it, not made it into a perfect mirror as well as showing imprinted within it a totally balanced self, then more work must be done to perfect it. To do this the Spirit self must again have access to the power of individuated consciousness through which it can perfect itself. The process by which the Spirit of a departed person can return to the Earth is that it must wait until a new soul, a new human being is created from the Divine, the life pattern of which will allow it the greatest opportunity to access the experiences and the consciousness that are needed to perfect its Immortal Spirit Body. In effect, what this means is that many of you actually have four selves, your own unique blend of the three selves of body, mind and soul as well as the self which is the Immortal Spirit self whose incomplete development you help to resolve. The best names for this Spirit that can attach itself to you before your physical involution is the 'Companion Spirit' or perhaps 'Overself.' In this case we could say that to some extent your life is a dual life. You have your own unique life possibilities to discover and side by side with this you are also influenced by the needs of your Companion Spirit. When the mirror of Spirit and the pattern imprinted within is perfected, the Immortal Spirit body perfectly formed; the

43

Companion Spirit will detach itself and finally move on to do work in other realms leaving you to develop your own unique Immortal Spirit self. This is not as parasitic a relationship as it probably sounds but a symbiotic one because you gain enormously in perception and understanding from the knowledge and experience gathered by your Companion Spirit in their original incarnation as a soul, body and mind.

Any imperfections in an Immortal Spirit Body nearly always manifest due to the problems and difficulties that arise in relationships, whatever their actual type or form, during the process of its creation. The development of the Spirit body is related to the flow of consciousness and its function as a connecting link within and between people. When a flow of consciousness can not complete its fundamental purpose, which is to carry information from one realm or one person to another and to have impact, the developing Spirit body is detrimentally affected. In life, any action creates a flow of different kinds of consciousness moving in a specific direction towards a certain goal or end. In a relationship one partner sends out consciousness towards the other who receives it, is affected by it, which in turn activates their awareness thereby generating more consciousness which then flows back. In essence the consciousness received from another person in life is fundamentally related to the content and impact of the consciousness sent out to them in the first place. This inter-relatedness continues for as long as there is a connection between the partners and remember this is a dual system as both partners are sending and receiving simultaneously.

This process can be blocked at virtually any point in the cycle. One partner can refuse to accept the flow of consciousness moving towards them by armouring themselves so as to shield against it. They can refuse to let it have any impact or transformative effect on them in any way, reflecting back a quality of consciousness that is untouched by and without reference to that which they initially received. They may stay out of awareness and thereby effectively block any return flow. In this same cycle, the sender can refuse to allow the return flow of consciousness to have any impact believing that it does not quite carry the desired response. Even at the very beginning of this whole process a partner can refuse to allow their consciousness to radiate by denying it any continuing awareness and attention thereby decreasing its potency.

The fundamental nature of consciousness is to move and to have impact. When this cannot happen it acquires a tension due to the enormous need for it to complete its pattern of flow. Its potential energy increases dramatically particularly if the awareness that created it is still active. It must complete its pattern of flow from the source to its intended goal, have impact there, thus creating some kind of transformation, which will in turn generate new awareness and consciousness which flows back to its trigger source again. To complicate the picture another aspect of the nature of consciousness is that it exists beyond time or independently of time. The vast increase in movement potential created by a blockage means that any incomplete pattern of flow of consciousness can achieve completion long after the blockage has occurred. It could take ten or twenty years after the movement of consciousness was initiated and in point of fact, completion could occur long after the people who created it are dead and buried, perhaps a hundred or a thousand years later because the consciousness not being bounded by space or time can wait as long as necessary for the perfect conditions, which would include the reincarnation of the Immortal Spirit selves of the people who generated it in the first instance.

An example should help to make all this clearer. Suppose some fifteen hundred years ago a couple had a close personal relationship and the man had an inability to actually express his love for the woman verbally, but instead expressed it through his actions. The woman however, had a great need for the man to express his love not just by his actions but also by saying that he loved her. As this situation continued for some time the woman, through the sheer frustration of never hearing him say "I love you," began to reject the meaning behind his actions. This effectively blocked the flow of consciousness that the man was sending out to her and arrested the development of both her Spirit body and his. Say this situation continued for a couple of years until they parted and then sadly a little while later she was killed and the man, grief stricken, commits suicide, thereby also finally arresting the development of his Immortal Spirit Body. In this scenario how are each going to attain the perfection of their Spirit body? The only way this can happen is for the Immortal Spirit selves of both the man and woman to return and join with other human beings once more. Not as their soul, body or mind but as their Companion Spirit. Thereby giving themselves the opportunity to create another relationship in which they can exchange consciousness and hopefully complete the work on their Spirit bodies as well as have the opportunity to work with the consciousness they created and left behind during their first and only true life on Earth.

For a person to be able to return to the Earth they must have ensured their own immortality. One of the soul's primary concerns is to achieve immortality through the creation of an Immortal Spirit Body, so as to always be able to permanently shine the light of love back to the source. If you have achieved even the most embryonic level of immortality then you can return and perfect your Spirit self. If not, all is lost. Indeed, it is possible that in a situation similar to the example above that only one person has ensured their immortality which means their task on return as a Companion Spirit is doubly hard though thankfully, not impossible.

Many spiritual teachings have a great deal to say on the subject of your life purpose. Your life purpose is usually seen to be synonymous with your soul purpose. Your soul is perceived to be incarnate to fulfil a specific purpose or to learn certain lessons. In our understanding your soul purpose is simply here to express love. However, for all of you, there are certain experiences which will allow better expression than others. In many instances it seems that life purposes are always seen in rather grandiose terms such as, for example, saving the world. The truth is life purposes are often much simpler than that; to be a loving parent, to be a chef, an architect, an artist or even perhaps a bank clerk. Banks have an interesting role to play in our modern world in that ultimately they nearly always provide the material resources required for people to manifest their dreams or their life purpose. Truly the list is endless. It is important not to get carried away on a wave of spiritual enthusiasm that degenerates into building castles in mid-air. You don't necessarily have to save or change the whole world to fulfil your life purpose. To change the world can only truly occur through individual personal action in your own unique world. That is, amongst your own relatives, friends and enemies. Even if it is your destiny to save the whole world you are not going to be able to do it without a few billion other people lending you their support through the realisation of their own much simpler, but nonetheless important, life purposes. Remember we all live in a great interlocking reality pattern every part of which must run smoothly for the whole to function properly.

Would you like to discover what your own life purpose is? Then study your own life up to this moment in time. What experiences have you had? What skills have you acquired along the way? What lessons have you learned? What things have you enjoyed doing the most? What makes you feel alive? Now imagine that someone else is telling you that all these answers are the pattern of what they have done and experienced in their life. Then looking at it from an outsider's perspective, tell them what life purpose you believe their soul has equipped them for and you have your own answer. Then try and live it. It won't necessarily be easy, though it might be. It may be an extraordinary new life adventure or you may already be doing it. What ever it is, please do not be tempted to try and judge its value because in all probability you will not be able to see its importance in the overall pattern of life on Earth. Be assured that it does fit and that it is important and essential. Surprisingly, simply the act of being born, living and then dying is a fulfilment of the most basic soul purpose, which is to exist and experience life. It will not ensure your immortality but it will support the rest of existence.

One of the paradoxes of following the power of love; of allowing your life to follow the power that is love; is that the shadows in your life, the areas in your life and being where the light of consciousness is lacking, are very often intensified. The path of love or of spiritual development could be characterised as being one of following the light within, the light of soul consciousness, the light that is love. However, light can only exist because there is also the possibility of its absence. Also consider that when you stand in the light that there is always a shadow of you somewhere. A place where the light is missing. The stronger the light, the deeper and more intense the shadows that are created.

In real human terms what does this concept of light and shadow mean? How does it manifest? It very often means that as much as you experience the love, so too, you come at some point to experience the opposite. A sombre period of emotional pain, fear, loss of faith, anger, jealousy and so on. It can all come at once so that one goes through what has been called the 'dark night of the soul.' However, more commonly it comes a little at a time so that periodically you experience blockages in your growth and your ability to follow the consciousness that is love. Confusion and temporary loss of heart is a common occurrence. There is no simple solution to these periods except to know that everything is governed by cycles and that if you can hold to the truth that shadows can only exist because there is light, then ultimately you will once more walk out into the light.

As you embrace the power of love and begin your journey through the light and the land of shadows, at times it is as if you are taken to the edge of a precipice below which is a vast canyon, symbolic of the life you have left behind. A life which was very often characterised by a lack of love and hope. A life in which your higher self was indeed the dweller in the dark. At times the urge to topple over is almost irresistible, to return to a less aware way of life, perhaps even to die. The reality of the situation is that once you have begun to be guided by the consciousness that is love you are never asked to endure more than you are capable of bearing. You are often taken right to the edge but you are never forced to jump off. The magnetic pull of the vast drop is awesome but you only have to turn aside. The times when you are brought to the edge of the precipice are always points at which you are able to make a breakthrough in your ability to deal with greater volumes of universal consciousness, provided you can just turn aside and walk on. The very first step away from the edge always fills you with a new vision. These periods are often ones of intense inner searching and self reflection. If one can just hold to the understanding that the light and shadow are mutually interdependent, and that it is the reality of life itself that makes the two a unity instead of a duality, then you will not be snared no matter how intense the shadows. What most of you need is a healing of the mental concept or belief of life as a duality; of mutually exclusive opposites, right and wrong, good and evil, black and white, hot and cold, love and hate. All of these terms are relative because in each case they are all about one thing not two.

At the other extreme, there comes a time in everyone's life when there is a perfect blend and balance of both inner and outer forces. A time when virtually all shadows are eliminated just as when the sun is directly over your head. This time is critical in a person's self transformation and the creation of their Immortal Spirit body. At this time whole new life directions can be set in motion, current problems and blockages are often powerfully resolved. This time has been called the time of fruition or fruitfulness. For many people it comes only once in a lifetime. For a very few it may happen twice or more. It is a time of rewards and an acknowledgement of that which went before as well as being the only true fresh start that you are ever given. It is certain that life and a person's sense of themselves is never the same after a time of fruition. The time of fruition is consecrated to God or more appropriately perhaps the 'All That Is.' From this time onward a person's life is no longer their own to direct. It is lived purely to serve life. This is also called the path of surrender which we will explore in more detail later in our discussion of the process of change. It is also the time of initiation.

It is possible when studying the understanding of reality espoused in this book to see that the universe of the soul is a relatively simple dimension, containing one substance that combines into different forms or souls. Yet when we look at the physical realm we see an extraordinary diversity of both fundamental elements and forms. Then, when we look at the mental dimension we see again a realm, like that of the soul, that contains one fundamental substance that combines into different forms. So we can postulate that there is an innate relationship between the soul and the mind and a similar relationship between the fourth dimension, that of the Divine and the physical realm. So, with the thought that your physical body could be a more intimate reflection of Divine consciousness than either your soul or your mind, let's look at it in more detail.

CHAPTER 3

THE BODY

Your body is the physical manifestation of your soul consciousness. The body plays a key role in your evolution into a truly human being due to the fact that there is no direct passage of soul consciousness and the information it carries, into the mental realm except via physical awareness and the creation of physical consciousness. Hence, your body stands between your soul and your mind and is the connecting link between them. The full and natural functioning of your physical body and the complete development of your awareness of it, is absolutely essential to your spiritual development. Your body is the perfect vehicle for your soul to express itself through in the physical dimension. The more involved you are in your body the more evolved you can become. To avoid or dissociate from the reality of your body in the slightest degree is to make yourself vulnerable to being caught in a mental illusion of your true evolutionary spiritual potential instead of the reality of it.

The appearance of soul consciousness in the physical realm triggers a number of events that ultimately culminate in the formation of a physical body. The first job of soul consciousness is to seek out the right parents in order to manifest. This it does through its ability to trigger sexual desire in the two people chosen, so as to bring them together physically to create a new life. There is no guarantee that sexual intercourse between two people on their first encounter will create new life so the sexual impulse continues to function until such time as the seed is sown, the egg fertilised, and a new life begun. There is a natural resonance between soul consciousness and physical sexual desire and attraction. Though that is not to say that all sexual desire is created by the need of a soul to manifest a physical form, the body itself needs sexual activity as part of its regulatory process and sometimes it is a more mental, ego centred need. In certain cases, the people upon whom the soul consciousness reacts will refuse, for various reasons, to act upon that impulse or desire. Should this be the case then the soul consciousness will, so to speak, move on and seek out other people through whom to manifest; people who will act out their sexual desire and help to create the physical form through which the soul can express itself. It is important to realise this link between sexual desire and soul consciousness is, in the first instance, a link which helps to create new life but is also a force that later in life brings people together into powerful intimate relationships. Relationships that may be vital for the needs of the new soul or so that the Companion Spirit can perfect its Immortal Spirit Body.

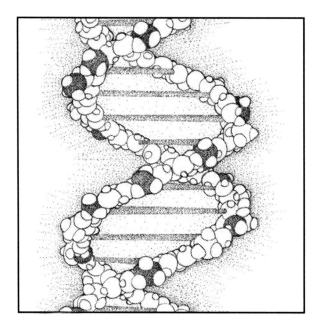

Figure 6

The information that is carried by soul consciousness is encoded into the physical equivalent of the soul pattern, the DNA molecule (Figure 6). The creation of a new DNA molecule requires the joining of a sperm and ovum through the act of physical lovemaking. The shape of the DNA molecule is, as we pointed out in the last chapter a double helix. Any derangement in the formation of the DNA molecule will have been caused by a disturbance of the passage of soul consciousness through the gateways during the early stages of the pregnancy. In very early life, when the child is still growing in the womb, much can be done to correct this problem by giving a soul body gateway clearance to the mother as described in the previous chapter. Treating the mother helps the child, because a child's soul body gateways are superimposed spatially over those of its mother as they emerge into the physical realm. Much can also be done just after birth using this technique, though it is important to remember that true contact areas for the various gateways are in fact not on the physical body of the young child. So, when doing such a treatment on a child, as you make physical contact with the various areas on their body remember that you are working on a microcosm of the true contact areas and that, through resonance, your work will affect the exact location of the gateways. You could of course work off the body at the actual location of the gateways but to do this accurately is difficult as you cannot be sure that your estimation of their exact position is correct. To get it right you have to be able to intuit the precise dimensions of the soul body of the child on whom you are working. If your connection with your own soul is very clear you might get it exactly correct, but it would not be necessarily any more effective than our first suggestion. Though we suspect many of you will not believe that, in which case you might like to do both. There is an excellent case to be made for all 'mothers to be' to receive a soul body gateway clearance, as described in the last chapter, regularly throughout pregnancy.

The DNA molecule is the basic or seed pattern for the construction of the physical body. In effect it draws the basic elements it requires for the formation of the cellular structure of the body from the mother initially and then later after birth directly from physical foods. The basic DNA pattern is replicated throughout the body in every single cell to ensure the continuity of form of the physical body throughout its life span. The microscopic seed pattern must be repeated in every cell because all the different kinds of interactions that occur between the many substances that make up the physical body require a local control system, unlike the soul body where there is only one substance that can be controlled by one single macrocosmic seed pattern.

As mentioned in the chapter on consciousness there are just two gateways in the physical body. One exists in the abdomen, specifically in the navel area, and one at the bask of the skull near the nape of the neck. The abdominal gateway is the one through which any consciousness that you generate from awareness of your physical body passes into the realm of the soul. Physical consciousness also passes through a gateway which is located at the back of your skull, near the organ at the base of your brain called the Medulla Oblongata (figure 7), from the physical into the mental dimension of your being. So, a full awareness of your physical body allows not just the passage of physical consciousness into the mental dimension but also into the universe of the soul. The location of your physical brain and the lower abdominal area are the two places in your physical body where consciousness tends to gather in large quantities before moving through into a different dimension of your being. Therefore, it is vitally important that physical consciousness is generated throughout your body otherwise there will be an incomplete exchange of information between the different dimensions of your being. Having only a partial awareness of your body, of only the head and upper torso for example, will mean that there is a good communication link between the physical environment that you live in and your mind but only partial contact with your body and hence a loss of contact with your soul. To be more specific, this lack of connection with the lower body means you are unaware of your feelings, the voice of your soul. Further, such a strong upper body-mind link also makes it difficult for you to send any information concerning the physical and mental worlds back to your soul. This gives rise to a situation which, in simple terms, can be stated as you not being able to reply to your soul because you did not even hear the question, thereby leaving your soul to work almost entirely in the dark. In a fully formed physical body the information carried to it via soul consciousness is to a large extent decoded in the lower pelvis; the physical seat of your feelings. Whereas, information carried to it by mental consciousness tends to be decoded in the head.

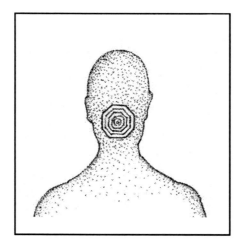

Figure 7

CLEARING THE PHYSICAL BODY GATEWAYS

Opening the gateway from the physical body to the mental realm can be done in many different ways. One of the easier techniques involves gentle movement of the head followed by a simple internal visualisation.

To begin just make yourself comfortable in a well supported sitting position. Then make small circles with your nose. The diameter of the circle should be between 1 and 2 inches or 3 to 4 centimetres. Imagine a clock face in front of you and make the movement of your nose clockwise around the face. Do it slowly and easily. Feeling the muscular adjustments in the back of your neck as you circle your nose. Continue this for two or three minutes. Then reverse the direction of the circle, making it anti-clockwise for about the same length of time. Now, at this point move your nose in semi-circles. Firstly from the 9 o'clock position through 12 o'clock to the 3 o'clock position and back again repeating this for about a minute and then secondly from 3 o'clock through 6 o'clock to 9 o'clock and back again, repeating this movement for the same length of time. All the time you are doing these movements you need to be aware of the muscular movement in the back of your neck particularly at the places where the muscles attach to the base of your skull. Now simply sit very still and experience the physical consciousness that you have generated in your head. To move it into the mental realm through the gateway at the base of your skull just visualise an octagonal opening appearing in the back of your head in the occipital area (figure 7) and sense all the consciousness disappearing through the opening. When you feel that all the consciousness has emptied out of your head through the gateway allow yourself to come gently back to everyday awareness.

To open the gateway between the physical body and the soul dimension begin by lying down in a comfortable position with your legs bent at the knees and feet flat on the floor. Place both hands palm down on your abdomen, take four slow, deep, easy breaths making sure that as you breath in you feel your abdomen expanding and are aware of your hands being pushed upwards toward the ceiling. Then very gently massage your abdomen easing any tension you feel in the area. Make the movements of your hands very soft and slow. Do this for about three minutes then take three more deep easy breaths again checking with your hands the expansion of your abdomen. Now do another abdominal massage this time for two minutes followed by two deep breaths and follow this by another massage of one minute's duration and a single deep flowing breath. Then simply lie and allow yourself to be aware of any movement in your abdomen. You may feel the pulsing of your abdominal aorta supplying blood to your lower limbs. At this stage see if you can imagine a point of light in your abdomen, a point of light that is growing steadily bigger and brighter until you have the sense that there is in fact a small sun in the centre of your abdominal cavity. Take a very deep breath, experiencing this small sun as moving upwards as your abdomen expands. Hold the breath in with the abdomen expanded for about 15 seconds then expel the air with a rush and as you do so imagine that the sun is sinking downwards inside you very rapidly, going down deeper and deeper until it has entirely disappeared from your awareness. Now you can just lie, relax and appreciate any internal sensations that you may be experiencing. Relax for as long as you like before returning to your normal level of awareness.

Once you have cleared the gateways you might like to try simply moving whilst you maintain a clear awareness of both physical body gateways. In fact, for most of you this will be a far from simple exercise. The majority of people walk through life with very little body awareness at all. Most move through the physical universe in a sort of dreaming state of mental awareness. You might find it helpful when experimenting with this exercise to try imagining the gateways as lit up like small suns as shown in figure 8. The fundamental purpose of the exercise is to create a continuous link between your mind and soul through your body during the whole of your waking life. Obviously the importance of this cannot be emphasised too much. Practise and work with the basic concept until it is not second but first nature. Use what ever form of imagery you need to facilitate the process.

If you are truly going to experience all that is joyful in your life on Earth then you must cultivate not just an awareness of the physical body gateways but a profound awareness of the whole of your body. It is only through a continuing and dynamic awareness of your body that you will be able to experience all the pleasure that having one offers. The more aware you are of your body the better the flow of movement within it and the healthier it will be. To become aware of your body is to become aware of all sensation both pleasant and unpleasant. In reality your bodily sensations cannot be described as either pleasant or unpleasant. These descriptions are a mental evaluation of any particular sensation. If you are to become fully aware of your body, you must begin the process of disentangling your mind and mental evaluation from your perception of the sensations in your body. In your quest to deepen your awareness of your body the one thing you must avoid is any labelling of your felt sense of your body as either good or bad, pleasant or unpleasant. Try and allow it to simply be what it is, just sensation.

The actual process of becoming aware of your body is closely akin to the exercising of your powers of imagination. This is because the feelings in your body are sometimes so subtle that you will often doubt the reality of your perception. You might find yourself thinking that you are imagining it all. However, physical awareness is both imagination and reality. True physical awareness is a passive perception of your body. Your mind should be still. Even with a still mind, your life energy still moves, your higher self and its own powers of thinking, information processing and imagination are still active. You could try and block this out, but it would be a

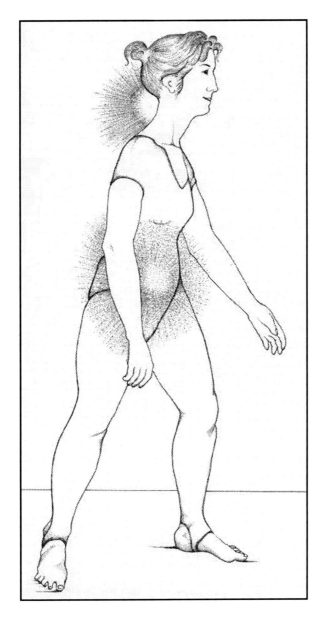

Figure 8

decidedly retrograde step to do so, particularly after all the soul body gateway clearance work you undertook in the last chapter! Awareness is something that should be cultivated throughout your entire life, in your every action and yet paradoxically there are also times when you should be completely unaware through total involvement with outer reality. So, do not focus too much on being 'in awareness' without balancing it by being 'without awareness.' Looking in should always be balanced with looking out. It is all to easy to become seduced by the power of looking in, by being too involved. We have said that you must involve fully in your body before you can evolve spiritually but the process of involution, of being in your body, must not become an addiction to the experience. Your awareness of your body is, if you like, the key that opens the door to your soul so that it can move out and express itself. However, the soul needs space to be able to do that, a constant involvement in your body is as if you are standing in the doorway that you have just opened, thereby effectively blocking it. This is why we say that there must be periods when you are unaware.

PHYSICAL BODY AWARENESS EXERCISE

To begin the growth of your awareness of your physical body you can use the following exercise, focusing on the subtle currents of breath that move through your body. Much of the movement in the physical body occurs due to cellular metabolism, the need for every single cell to have oxygen and eliminate carbon dioxide. Oxygen is absorbed from the breath and carried into the blood stream through which it is distributed to every part of the body by the diffusion of the blood. You will need at least twenty minutes to complete this exercise. You also need to ensure that you will not be disturbed by any external influences as you do it.

Find yourself a comfortable position in which you can lie down and simply breathe. As you breathe just allow yourself to become aware of any sensations in your body. Try to maintain an even steady breathing pattern. The process of becoming aware of all the different sensations in your body as you gently and easily focus on your breathing means that you begin to internalise; to look inwards and see within, literally to have internal eyes and indeed internal ears. In fact, all the senses can be turned inwards instead of being habitually focused outward.

Many people have pointed out how important it is to be in touch with your feelings and your body. The concept of being 'in touch' is an extremely apt phrase. Fundamentally, that is all there is to this body awareness exercise. As you repeat it over a period of time do not be surprised if the intensity of the feelings that you experience increases enormously.

There are many different kinds of sensations within your body that relate to its physiological functioning such as hunger, thirst and cellular repair work. These sensations arise specifically within the physical body itself and are due to action specific to the physical realm only. They are not connected to your experience of your soul, or the impact of soul consciousness on your physical body. They include muscular movement, pressure, the pulsation of your internal organs and all the different kinds of pain that you can experience. An actual descriptive list of all the sensations possible would be almost infinitely variable due to the unique quality of personal experience, and we feel sure that you can easily add to the ones that we have just described. Do not limit yourself to just working with an awareness of your breath as described above. In movement, be aware of your muscles. In stillness, be aware of your skin. As another exercise see if you can learn to distinguish between those sensations that arise in your body due to the action of your soul, or indeed your mind, from those that only originate in your body and the physical realm.

It is difficult for you to get to know your body self and its reactions to your life unless you can be clear as to which sensations originate solely in your physical body. However, it must be said that any pain or physical illness you are currently experiencing will tell you a great deal about the opinions of your body self. However, pain and illness are really very intense reactions upon the part of your body and mind to attract your mental attention to the fact that there is a major problem in or with certain aspects of your life. We feel that it is important to point out here that under normal conditions your physical body is never disturbed in any way by the impact of, or effect of soul consciousness, and the life of the soul in general. There is a situation when this is not the case but it only occurs in extreme circumstances and the kind of physical problem that arises is always of a life threatening nature, such as cancer. We will have much more to say about this situation, but not until later on in the last chapter of this book. What the body self reacts to with pain and physical illness is generally the actions of your ego and your mental world. Though, of course, there are experiences that originate in the physical dimension alone, such as slipping on a banana skin! That will definitely create pain in your body and a strong reaction in your body self.

TALKING WITH YOUR BODY-SELF

To discover your body-self reactions or thoughts concerning your life all you need to do is pose it some specific questions and listen to the answer. For example, say you want to discover what this particular self thinks about your current occupation. Simply sit down in a comfortable position and allow yourself to relax as much as possible and get a sense of the physical tension level in your body and also observe your breathing rate and volume. Then engage your mind in some simple repetitive action like counting from zero to 100 in two's for about a minute so as to block off any particular 'thoughts' that might interfere with the process. Now simply ask you body, silently in your mind, if it likes your present job and then be aware of any shift in your bodily sensations, which is its reply to your question. If you experience no change in either tension or your breathing rate then the answer is non-committal. It is acceptable. However, if you experience a sudden tightening in the muscles in one part of your body, or if you are aware that you take a much deeper breath and let it go with a heavy sigh, then the answer is "No." It does not like it for some reason. On the other hand, if you feel a sudden relaxation of some part of your musculature, or if you find that you take a slow, deep breath in and out, then the answer is "Yes." At this point with the answers you have you can refine your questioning to elicit further more detailed information.

The language of the body is essentially movement. To be more specific, it is expansion and contraction. Any general feeling of warmth, expansion and relaxation in the body is a positive response. Whereas any feeling of cold, contraction or tightening in the body is a negative response. Positive responses are also generally slow and steady changes in sensation and negative responses usually quick and abrupt. It is possible to verify the meaning of your own body language by asking a series of questions the answers to which you know already. All body selves enjoy good food, warm beds and adequate sleep so just ask some simple "yes" or "no" questions concerning these areas, and by being aware of the physical changes you will have a pretty good idea of how your body self communicates.

Of all the sensations that having a body allows you to experience, pain is perhaps the most fascinating and interesting. It does not exist as a tangible measurable substance. It is, in essence, a value judgement in your mental being concerning the consciousness that arises from your awareness of the sensations you experience, through your physical nervous system in relation to some form of stimulation. What is painful to one person is not to another. The difference lies in the mind not in the body. Pain is a signal that you experience when either your body or mind come under some form of pressure. The nature of the pressure may be external or internal. It can arise from something someone says to you, from a physical blow, gas pains, or unrestricted cellular growth in your body, or some form of mental or emotional conflict within you. Sometimes the pain of living becomes so great that people commit suicide to escape it. Unfortunately, they also thereby lose the opportunity to experience all the pleasure that life can also offer, as well as curtailing the development of their Immortal Spirit. However, it is possible to ease your pain without such extreme measures and to do so requires that we look at the other side of pain which is pleasure.

If you think about it, your body allows you to feel pleasure in so many things; the taste of your favourite food, the satisfaction of a full stomach, the smell of fresh sea air, the visual beauty of a glorious sunrise, the touch of someone you love, the joy of making love, the ecstasy of orgasm. The list will be different for each of you and the variety is limitless. Pleasure is an interesting subject because, just like pain, it too, is a value judgement in the mind concerning the sensations that you experience through your nervous system in relation to some form of stimulation. In fact, it can also occur when you experience some form of pressure. Most people at some point in their lives have felt that they could just explode with happiness. What about the sensation experienced in anticipation of a good meal after finishing a diet of some kind. Is that pain or pleasure or even a pleasurable pain? Sexual excitement is an intense form of stimulation that most find extremely pleasurable, and yet, is it not also a pressure that can be painful as well? Just reflect for a few moments on all the things that you personally find pleasurable. Could they not also, at a certain level of intensity, be said to be painful also? What about the things you find painful? Are they not also pleasurable in some sense, particularly if you focus on the actual sensation that you experience without making any mental judgements? We are not saying that there is no difference at all between pain and pleasure, but that the dividing line is very thin. With a little exploration of your own experience and a slight adjustment to your thinking, you could eliminate a great deal of your pain and increase your potential for joy enormously. Alternatively you could eliminate a great deal of your pleasure and increase your pain enormously. It's just as easy and many people in fact do just this.

It is difficult to maintain a link with your higher self when you are in a lot of physical or mental pain, so it would be of benefit to decrease your pain and increase your joy. Go on, try it, let your soul sing through your body! However, we must also say that all pain is not something that you should try and eliminate entirely, particularly when it relates to your physical body. Pain is your early warning system. It tells you when to get out of the way, when the pressure your physical body is experiencing is too great to be borne safely. However, there is no reason not to seek to eliminate or reduce the chronic on-going pain that accompanies physical damage which cannot, for some reason, heal properly. You should explore your pain in depth. What kind of pain is it? What is its cause? Can you influence your experience of it? What is it telling you? Make it your friend and it will become a most extraordinary teacher.

The ultimate awareness exercise is to become aware of the whole of your being and consciousness all at the same time. Indeed, that is the key to all the material in this book and the development of your Immortal Spirit. Spiritual development, the evolution of your Immortal Spirit Body, is basically a natural process that begins as soon as you become fully involved in your physical body. To be fully involved in your body is to allow your soul consciousness to infuse it fully and completely, as well as to have full physical awareness of it. This tends to happen naturally as you come to love and appreciate your body as being the image of your soul. The body is the physical manifestation of the soul. It is the perfect vehicle for the soul to express itself through. The actual shape and structure of it is governed by the soul consciousness that emanates from your higher self.

There is an important question that we need to consider when looking at the human body from a soul level perspective, and that question is: "why do you have a body?" The answer is that you have a body so as to enable your soul to experience and interact with the physical world. The human body is essentially a device for the transformation of consciousness. Having a physical body allows you to transform one form of consciousness into another. The body is also an energy transformer that is capable of transforming the biophysical energy obtained from food, air, and sunlight into motor activity. To be able to transform energy implies that you have access to it in all its various forms, so that you can then transform it through the action of your body and your awareness. You are a soul, a body and a mind so that you can experience all levels of existence, from the most mundane physical levels to the most sublime soul levels, and more importantly so you can have fun!

The transformation of matter and consciousness are pleasurable experiences of the highest order. The fact that you have a body gives you the ability to experience the physical realm in intimate detail. It gives both your soul and mind the chance to experience action in the physical dimension of existence. Furthermore, remember that the physical universe is a closer analogue of the realm of the Divine than either the soul or mental dimensions of existence. So your body can be said, in a certain sense, to be closer to God than any other aspect of your being. Your ordinary, very far from mundane physical body is, strange though it may seem, the key to your immortality. It is also in itself a remarkable reflection of the Creator. So if you would know God, seek out the reality of your physical body. Young children offer us the best example of what a body is like when it is full of love—full of pleasure. When the connection with the soul, the higher self is still clear, there is literally a quality of vibrancy about the body; a visible glow or radiance. The muscles are soft and full, rather as if they are filled with air. The posture is balanced and erect. Children, as any parents will know, have boundless energy. They can play or cry for hours without getting tired. Having said this, we know that there are young children that are not as we have described them. This is because the degree of contact with the higher self varies even for very young children. Many factors enter in to this, mainly in the form of the destructive mental and emotional conditioning that parents, relatives, school teachers, and society in general inflict upon them. That your body could, and should, have these qualities as an adult is one of the things that is meant in spiritual teachings when it is said that you should become as little children again. It is a major step in your spiritual development.

If you are physically ill or if you feel negative in any way about the body that you have, then you are experiencing a lack of love in, and for, your body. Remembering that the soul is the source of love within you, we could also say that you are losing contact with your soul. Your body is not being fully infused with your soul consciousness. You can strengthen your contact with your soul either by mentally deciding to love yourself more or by deepening your level of contact with your soul or higher self. Different routes that create the same effect—a return to wholeness. Your soul is always working to guide you to the do things that will help you to love yourself more, that will give you a better integration between all the levels of 'beingness' that go to make you fully human. Carl Jung, the famous psychoanalyst, called this phenomena the 'self-regulating nature of the psyche.' It is one of the practical ways in which the soul uses the power of love.

At any time in your life when you begin to feel bad about your body because you think that it is the wrong shape, size or colour, you are limiting the amount of joy that you could be having. To have fun in life you have to be involved in life, in your physical body. You need to experience it to the full and yet if you feel bad about your body, you almost always begin to think that other people share in your opinion about it. Once you begin to think that way, you will in all probability begin to avoid people. You will stop going out in to the world. As soon as that happens you are not having fun any more. Inevitably, few people love their body as much as they could or as much as it deserves. Almost all of you will have had the experience of looking at yourself some days and thinking how good you feel, and how good your body looks. If you think back to such a time, or the next time you have that experience, ask yourself what the subjective experience of your body is. We can almost guarantee that somehow the feelings were of being bigger or more expanded. A very real sense of filling up your own space and of being at home in your own skin. This is the tangible kinaesthetic experience of soul consciousness impacting upon your physical body. The nature of soul consciousness is love, so at such moment, we could say that you are filled with love.

It is possible to make this sense of your body more of an everyday occurrence by simply loving yourself more. A piece of advice often given by many teachers of the art of living, but for most people we know that this is very difficult to put into practise. The greatest difficulty being that for many, love is little more than a 'word concept' that defines a certain kind of behaviour and feeling towards another person. The key to part of your difficulty lies in the words 'other person' in that you are taught that your love is to be given only to another person and that if you want to experience love it must come from someone else loving you. It should not be something you do for yourself because that implies an unhealthy narcissism. Sadly, there are many other cultural and ideological beliefs about love that have a detrimental effect on you ever being able to love yourself fully. We will have much more to say on the subject of love later in the book when we explore relationships.

One of the practical techniques that is often recommended as a way of loving yourself more is to actually do more of the things that you know you enjoy and that make you feel good. As a method of proving that you do love yourself it has some real validity, except that for many people it somehow feels like they are simply being selfish and over indulgent. In the long run this can engender feelings of guilt which are totally counterproductive. Another technique is the use of positive affirmations, simply repeating to yourself a particular sentence stating in some way how much you love yourself or some part of yourself. The idea being, that done often enough, it will create a shift in the emotions you experience about yourself, because the constant repetition becomes a learning process that affects you on a level outside your everyday awareness. It gives you positive beliefs about yourself that counteract any negative ones held in your mind. However, for the technique to be fully effective the consciousness generated by the pattern of the new belief must be powerful enough for it to supplant the old. If it is not, then it will have no effect because the old belief is too strong. If they are of equal strength a conflict will be set up in the mind that cannot be resolved. A conflict, which in itself, can set up other secondary problems. As a technique it works well for some people but for others it seems as though they are basically lying to themselves, which negates the effect of the affirmation because it reduces the amount of consciousness generated by the new belief.

We are going to offer you a technique that is based on the effect of soul consciousness on the rest of your being as well as the idea that your mental self image, the emotions you experience in relation to your body, are held in a part of your mind that is outside your everyday awareness. It works through the fact that one of the main ways these parts of your mind communicate is through patterns that symbolise reality in an abstract way, rather than with direct representations of the actual things themselves. It is a very simple but powerful way of coming to love yourself more.

ENFOLDING YOUR BODY IN LOVE

Before you begin please make sure you have at least twenty minutes of free time during which you will not be disturbed. Then get a friend to give you one of the soul body gateway clearance sessions as described in chapter 2. Once this is completed your partner will then talk you through the rest of the process in the following way. They will begin by asking you to decide on the part of the body that you want to work on, the part that you want to love, to connect your soul consciousness with. They will then ask you to imagine something that would symbolise or represent that particular part of your body and ask you to hold that image in your mind's eye. Next, they will ask you to add something to the image you are holding in your mind. Once you have done this they will ask you to take something away from the double image. At this point they will ask you to imagine something that would represent Love. They will then tell you to join the symbol of the part of your body to the symbol you have for love in such a way that it is a dynamic image, that there is a definite sense of interaction between the two symbols. Finally they will tell you to allow the image to sink downwards inside you, getting smaller and smaller as it drifts down deep inside you until it is completely gone from view. When you are ready you can then come back to normal everyday awareness.

If you do not have someone who can give you a soul body gateway clearance the whole process can be done on your own by substituting the following technique. It will get you in to the appropriate state of awareness without any external aid.

Sit or lie down in a comfortable position and close your eyes. Raise both hands directly above your head so that your finger tips touch about 18 inches or 45 centimetres above the top of your head, in your transpersonal gateway. Take an easy breath in and as you breath out allow your hands to drop down and touch your throat area with your finger tips. Take another easy breath in and as you breath out drop your hands so that the fingers of your left hand touch your left shoulder gateway and the right touch the right shoulder gateway. Take another easy breath in and as you breath out drop your hands so that the finger tips of your left hand touch your left breast gateway and the right touch the right breast gateway. Take another easy breath in and as you breath out lower your hands and touch the spleen gateway with your left finger tips and your liver gateway with your right finger tips. Take another easy breath and then as you breath out drop both hands down onto your lower pelvic area. Rest for a little while breathing slowly and easily, then on an in breath raise your hands and touch the liver gateway with your right finger tips and your spleen gateway with your left finger tips and breath out. On the next in breath raise your hands and touch your right breast with your right fingers and your left breast with your left. On the next in breath raise your hands and touch your right shoulder with your right finger tips and your left shoulder with your left finger tips. On the next in breath raise both hands and touch your throat lightly with the fingers of both hands. Then on the next in breath raise your hands and touch your finger tips together in the transpersonal gateway. Now, slowly allow your hands to fall outwards in front of you as you continue to breath slowly and easily until they are floating in front of your solar plexus and finally bring them slowly towards you until you can place both hands palm down over your solar plexus. At this point you can continue with the process that comes after the gateway clearance as outlined above. If you find all the instructions too difficult to remember you can record this whole process on tape and then relax as you talk yourself through it.

In essence the technique is very simple. As an example, suppose you feel bad about the shape and size of your abdomen. Follow the technique for doing the exercise on yourself as just described and at step three you begin to think about your abdomen and see if you can think of something that would represent it in your mind's eye. In this case we will say that you get the image of it as a brown cardboard box. Holding this image of the cardboard box in your mind just add something to it. Let us say a pencil appears. You now have a cardboard box and a pencil in your mind's eye. At this point allow something to disappear from this double image. In this case it is the cardboard box that disappears leaving you with just the image of the pencil. Now think about your concept of love. What would you chose as a symbol representing Love? Let us say you see love as white light. Now you simply join the two images that you have together in your mind's eye. In this case you see the pencil and then shine white light on it until it is surrounded with light. You want this to be a dynamic image so that the effect of this visualisation can continue after you have let the images go and in this case you allow yourself to see that the source of the white light is a light bulb, or something similar, that it is plugged into a mains socket which you leave switched on, thereby giving yourself the idea that this is a continuing process. Then you simply allow the image to sink downwards inside you, getting smaller until it has disappeared completely. Finally, simply lie still for a while noticing the sensations in your body and then when you fee ready, just open your eyes and get on with your everyday life.

The reason for adding something to the image of the body part that you are working on is to access anything else that at some deeper level of your mind might be the real symbol for that part of you which is experiencing a lack of love. In other words, a more appropriate symbol. If nothing extra appears when you try to add something to the image of the body part you working on, then proceed immediately to combine it with your symbol for love. Allowing something to disappear from any double image that appears is to clarify where you should be applying your love, your soul consciousness, to best effect. When something disappears from the double image you might find that the object you added is what goes or, as in the previous example, the first image. It may also happen that only a part of one of the images may disappear. Whatever happens the rule is to work with whatever is left.

In the example, the need to leave the light plugged in occurred because the symbol for love was an active symbol rather than a passive one. Light needs to be created continuously because its speed of movement means it would only interact with your other symbol for as long as you shone it upon the image with direct attention. Without providing a continuous source of light, as soon as you let the image go, the object would be plunged back into darkness and the light that you created would speed off into the infinite expanse of your being. A passive image for love would be something like a soft blanket—an image whose effect would obviously continue to function without your direct attention because it is a static object. Once created and placed around your other symbol it has to continue interacting with it because it cannot move of its own accord. It is not important whether your symbol for love is an active or a passive one. They are both equally effective. Please do not be tempted to use any particular archetypal image for love that you have read, or been told about. Only use symbols that appear spontaneously in your awareness in relation to the particular body part that you are working with. What is important is that the image is your own and do not be surprised if you get some really odd symbols occasionally. If you use the technique more than once you may find that over a period of time your symbol for love changes. Always use any new symbol that arises, not the old. Remember that change is a constant and natural part of life.

The shift in your own feelings about whatever part of your body you are working on will occur within a week of you doing the visualisation. You may also frequently get a normalisation of either the size or functioning of the body part in question, though this can take longer. The actual amount of time depends on your own physiology and metabolism. You may find that when you practise this technique that you fall asleep towards the end of the exercise or even earlier. Do not worry about this. Simply repeat the technique when you are feeling more rested. The quality of awareness that arises at the boundary between wakefulness and sleep is a very useful one so do not be surprised if you find staying awake difficult when doing any of the less physically active exercises in this book. It is also possible to use this technique on aspects of your sense of self or your personality that you feel need more love. Simply think of the particular quality that you want to work on and see what symbol you get then proceed as you did above. It can be a valuable tool when trying to change your mind and emotions.

Human beings are definitely not static phenomena so how do you use your body? Do you use and infuse your physical actions with love? For many people their bodies are dull, heavy, almost lifeless objects that they drag through life with great effort. To feel love for your body is important, but it is just as important to experience the joy of being in the movement, that is your body. Your body is full of movement, heart beat, blood flow, breathing, interstitial fluid movement, peristalsis, and so on, even when, outwardly, it is at rest. How do you move? How do you eat, talk, make love, walk, run, play? Do you play with your body even as a child will play with theirs, taking great delight in exploring all the different possibilities for movement that it offers? Do you ever think of feeling your body as you move? How does it feel to walk? Is it a pleasurable experience for you? Remember we have already said that having a body allows you to experience pleasure but this is not limited to a static appreciation of your physical form and the sensory experience that it offers through touch, taste, smell, vision, and hearing. You actually have one other major sense—the kinaesthetic sense of your body. The true sixth sense. The kinaesthetic sense is your inner felt experience of, and in, your body, and its spatial relationship to its environment. To really feel your body in movement is a love filled and beautiful experience. If you judge your movement capabilities as inept, clumsy or disjointed then you are denying yourself the joy of feeling all movement as simply movement, as 'life.' In fact, if you do make these kind of judgements about yourself then you have obviously never been fully aware of your movements. To be in the body and to feel totally its movements is to have no space in your mind for value judgements concerning their quality. This is due to the sheer amount of awareness that functions purely in your physical body and the enormous volume of physical consciousness that then floods you mental body. To just be in the movement, indeed to be in anything totally, is to be in love—to be one with you soul.

Your body is not a solid object. It is movement and vibration and, as such, has no limitations on its ability to change except those imposed by your mind with its many beliefs. The truth is that whatever shape your body is in at this moment it is in essence, in its core, a manifestation of the love that is your soul consciousness. So, it is always perfect as it is. Yet because it is movement it is always changing its form, sometimes so subtly as to be invisible but changing nevertheless. You could say that at all times you move from perfection to perfection. You have to change because movement is change. Without change life is unthinkable; without any movement your physical body is dead.

We are beings who walk within the radiance of Love, within the manifestation of your soul consciousness. In reality you are always in love. You all know what it feels like physically when you are in love. In that first glow of love your body feels weightless and expanded. You feel joyous and it seems, when you move, as if you are walking on air. Your movements become effortless and fluid. You are in, and experiencing your physical form more intensely than at any other time. You feel light because you are both receiving and expressing the light that is love, that is soul consciousness. Yet this feeling is your birthright, regardless of whether or not you are in relationship to any other, because when your soul consciousness is being generated and expressed you are constantly moving and being in love all the time! To know and express the nature of your soul through your body is to be involved in one of the greatest love affairs there is. An affair that is always new. When this happens you can be as constantly radiant as you were during your very first true love affair.

WALKING IN THE PRESENCE OF LOVE

One of the simplest ways of experiencing this quality of movement is to practise what we also call 'light walking.' This is simply walking as if you are in love. To do this all you have to do is walk whilst imagining that you have just fallen in love. Your mind will provide you with the specifics from your own memory as to how you actually felt physically at that time. Even if you have never been in love with another person it is almost certain that you have deeply loved something in life, perhaps an animal, and that you can access that feeling. The object of your love may vary but the feelings are the same. Love is love. As you do this it is almost certain that you will see and experience the world in quite a different way to normal. Objects may seem brighter. Time may seem to speed up or slow down. You may literally feel bigger. The movement might seem effortless, or you could also simply feel suddenly joyful. The list is probably endless but all of you will experience some if not all of these characteristics.

The ease and freedom of movement that occurs during 'light walking' is directly related to the feeling of expansion. As the physical body is basically composed of atoms and molecules held at a certain spacing, which vibrate at different frequencies, the sense of expansion is in actual fact a subtle felt sense of an actual physical increase in the spacing between the atoms and molecules in your body. We are only talking about microns of actual expansion at this level, but it is significant because much of the time your atoms, molecules, and cells are just fractionally too close for the optimum functioning of the whole system. As an analogy, most of you will have seen what happens when a washing machine that is not fitted properly, or one whose load is unbalanced, does when it goes into its spin cycle. It will literally move across the floor. If you apply pressure to it by sitting on it or bearing down on it with your hands, which is essentially the application of a compressive force, the movement stops. The movement stops because the frictional forces between the washing machine and the floor increase to a level where movement is impossible. As a by-product, a good deal of destructive heat is also created. A similar process happens in the human body through the collapse that occurs when you are out of touch with the love of your soul. The atoms and molecules become compressed and the innate movement capacity of the body decreases noticeably. A great deal of internal friction and stress is created in various parts of the body which gives rise to excessive heat production locally in these areas. All of which drastically impedes the natural functioning and healing capabilities of the body. This compression of the cellular and atomic structure of the body is the real source of many physical problems. The adequate functioning of the body cannot occur when there is compression and, behind this, a lack of love. The reason that the exercise in which you send love to certain body parts often normalises the function of that particular area, is because the love or soul consciousness will cause an expansion of the cells and atoms thereby creating the ideal conditions for optimum metabolism. When you are experiencing your soul through the light of consciousness your whole being expands. Your physical body vibrates more intensely and spontaneous movement begins to occur. To go where you wish all you have to do is direct that innate vibratory movement. It is also the essence of the body's anti-gravity capability. Love gets you upright and helps you to stay there! After all, how many times have you thought of love as being supportive!

Here is a small secret. In many of the teachings based upon ancient traditional wisdom such as that of the North or South American Indian cultures, much is made of the shaman's ability to penetrate into other 'realities.' These other realities are not somewhere other than where your physical body exists now. They are not fantastic creations of a mind influenced by narcotics, no matter how seductive these experiences may be. The actual usage of a narcotic is to simply prove how fallible mental perceptions can be, and to break up the belief in there being only one indivisible dimension to existence. There are other dimensions to existence, an infinite number in fact, but human beings only exist in three; those of the body, mind and soul. It is virtually irrelevant from any healing perspective to be able to enter any dimensions other than these as they hold no great value for the healing of human problems. The truth is that the most important reality that a shaman must be able to enter into is the true 'physical reality' that you all exist in but that your mind does not allow you to see. The actual nature of physical reality is awesome, majestic and full of miracles. There are enfolded mysteries within it. It is a realm of enormous power where things are both less solid and yet more substantial than you can imagine. The physical realm is vastly and fundamentally different from your everyday mental perceptions of it. The most direct way to reach a valid perception of it, indeed perhaps the only true way, is to focus deeply on your physical body. This is the real path of the shaman.

Too many people see the body as the animal part of man. It is considered to be base, low or that part of man which indicates his fall from Grace. These people will never find God nor develop an Immortal Spirit because they don't look low enough. A true taste of God, the All That Is, isn't up out there somewhere. It is down here in there, in your body. It is real, it has nothing to do with the 'higher' mental aspirations of man. It is down here on the Earth, in your body. Some of the major world religions say that man was created in the image of God, but God created the soul first to be his messenger and then the soul created the physical body in the likeness of God. The next stage in the creation process occurs when the physical body creates the mind. A mind that is in fact, created in the image of the soul. You probably think this sounds highly improbable. So, lets explore the mind and find out.

CHAPTER 4

THE MIND

One of your biggest problems and your greatest gifts is the power of your mind. The mental dimension of your existence is as vast as the physical universe. Your imagination, which can roam freely throughout your mental universe in an instant, is capable of creating anything within this realm. In your own unique mental world you are as a god. This vast power can be used to create great good in all of the different dimensions of your being or evil. Your mind which is itself an aspect of your mental body and your mind self or ego are fundamentally there to facilitate the needs and requirements of both your body and soul. Sadly, it seems many people believe that the body is created to serve the needs and wants of the mind and they are not even certain there is such a thing as the soul. If this is true for you then your mind is certainly not serving the life principle.

The mental body is created after the creation of the physical body. The basic requirement for the creation of the mental body is for physical consciousness emanating from the physical brain to pass into the mental plane of existence. This only begins to happen in quantity after physical birth and the opening of the five senses to both the inner physical world of bodily sensations and the outer world of the physical Earth. As soon as physical consciousness appears in the mental plane of existence the information that it carries is encoded into the basic stuff of the mental universe in the form of a double spiral. In esoteric traditions its name varies from the Caduceus energy pattern and the Staff of Hermes to the Ida and Pingala as it is referred to in the Indian yogic tradition and is sometimes represented as two intertwined serpents. It is this pattern which is the source of your mental body (Figure 9). It is the 'mind pattern' or mental body spiral and because of its shape it has a natural resonance with the soul pattern and the physical DNA pattern, all three patterns being double helixes. The mind pattern, once created, gathers around it sufficient of the basic element of the mental universe to create the mental body. The mental body should have exactly the same shape as the physical body. Frequently, because its formation takes place over the whole of the physical growing phase from birth to physical maturity, a period of

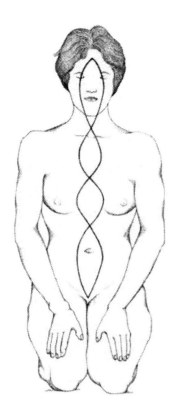

Figure 9

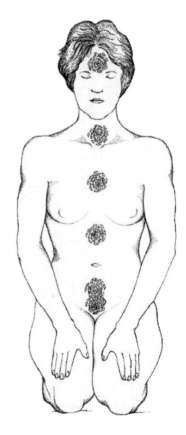

Figure 10

72

between eighteen and twenty five years, and because the consciousness upon which it is based is not always very clear the mental body does not always match the physical form. Distortion also occurs because the mental body must change just as the physical body changes. Should there be any disturbance of the continuous movement of physical consciousness into the mental dimension of being throughout life then problems will arise due to the mental body being encoded with imperfect information. Distortion can also manifest due to problems within the mental body itself. The main problem being due to distorted patterns of thinking that interfere with the ability of the mind stuff to bond together in the appropriate fashion, preventing the construction of an exact mental body.

The mental body is composed, as we said, of mind stuff which is the basic element of the mental universe. The fundamental property of mind stuff is that it is easily bound into complex shapes or patterns by the action of the mind pattern as well as both physical and mental consciousness to create 'thought forms.' Thought forms are the embodiment in the mental realm of the information carried by consciousness. Thought forms can be extremely durable structures which can survive for hundreds, or perhaps even thousands of years, of physical time provided their structure is sufficiently stable and balanced and also that they are not eaten by someone! Don't worry, you will understand what we mean by that later when you have finished reading this chapter. However, the stability of the thought forms created by mental consciousness is dependent upon the function of the mind pattern. It is that which moulds their outer structure or shell into the appropriate pattern in the first instance. Small thought forms, and most are, do not need their own integral mind pattern to gain durability. Only very large patterns like the mental body have that requirement. Keeping the gateway at the base of the skull open thereby allowing free passage of physical consciousness into the mental realm is essential to the continuing function and existence of the mind pattern.

It is in fact possible for the mental body of a person to survive both the death of the physical body and the dissolution of the soul body. However, in no way could this be seen to be the creation of an immortal mental body. Immortality is not a possibility within the mental realm. The durability of a large thought form like the mental body is dependent upon the existence of a sustaining mind pattern within it. A mind pattern can only be created by the appearance in the mental universe of physical consciousness emanating from a physical body. A great deal of mental effort and emotional need, coupled with an absolute faith in the power of the mind, does allow a person so inclined to stabilise their mind pattern so that their mental body can survive after death

73

but it will only be for a limited time span. At a certain point it will begin to disintegrate into the simple un-patterned mind stuff of the mental universe once more. Furthermore, the kind of existence thus achieved is only within the mental plane of existence and actually forms the basis of the phenomenon commonly referred to as ghosts. A pseudo-immortal mental body can only exist within the mental dimension and because it cannot communicate with the other dimensions of reality, having no physical or soul bodies of its own, it is also the basis of the phenomena of possession. Possession occurs when a mental body that has survived the death of the physical body that helped to create it tries to borrow someone's physical form to communicate with the other dimensions of existence. We are sure that you can think of many other unusual phenomena that can be accounted for by the existence of mental bodies that have achieved a degree of durability within their own dimension. We also hope that it is clear to you that this process is not true spiritual development. The real immortal spirit body is truly indestructible and has contact with all dimensions of reality. The mental body and mind self are but one part of the whole human being. Albeit a part that must be mastered and developed but also most importantly, integrated with the rest.

Once your physical body has achieved maturity and reached its full stature, it does not stop growing but the continuing growth is in the repair and maintenance of its structure. In the mental plane of your being it is also usual for your mental body to cease growing once it has achieved equivalent maturity in relation to your physical body. The nature of the element of which the mental body is composed is not prone to deterioration in the same way that the elements that compose your physical body are, so it does not need to repair and maintain itself in the same way as the physical body. However, should your mental body not reflect in some way the continuing and subtle growth, repair and ultimately decay that is always taking place in the physical realm then the one to one correspondence between the two bodies is lost. This is why people often say when they are seventy years old that inside they still feel the same as when they were twenty or thirty. In this situation their physical body is seventy years old but their mental body is still reflecting the body they had when they were perhaps twenty or thirty. Many problems can occur in such a person's ability to adapt to the changing needs and abilities of their physical body. In this particular scenario the mind and mental body often ask and expect more of the physical body than it can possibly deliver. A mental body that is not continually changing and growing within its overall pattern can also be the basis of the kind of rigidity that is so common in human beings after reaching physical maturity. The mental body must grow and change or else it becomes rigid. The feedback loops between the physical and mental dimensions are then unbalanced and ultimately the physical body will itself tend to become stiff and rigid as the force of the mental consciousness emanating from the awareness of a fixed, tight, and rigid mental body impacts upon it.

When awareness or spirit is active in your mental body then the mental consciousness generated passes back into the physical dimension through six gateways that are, as we mentioned in the first chapter, commonly referred to in many esoteric and magical traditions as the 'chakras.' Curiously, many of the current concepts of spiritual development seem to revolve around the clearing of any obstructions to the passage of mental consciousness through the six chakras. However, what this can ultimately lead to is little more than the development of a kind of mental concept of spiritual development. That is to say a person who has worked for many years on clearing their chakra system and honing their mental consciousness may well think that they have achieved a good degree of spiritual development but unfortunately, this is not the case. The operative word here is 'thinks.' The development that they have achieved is often within the mental dimension only. They often ignore the needs of the physical body and in learning to control their mental-emotional state they loose contact with the essence of the soul which is pure feeling; feeling that is always carried to the mind via physical consciousness and the body. What we are saying is that you must clear all of the gateways in each of your three bodies as well as achieve mastery of each dimension of your being and finally establish an integration between all three. This is the only way that you can create an immortal spirit. Focusing entirely upon the mental body and mind self can only lead to a partial kind of spiritual development.

The actual location of the mental body gateways (or chakras) in relation to your physical body are shown in Figures 10 and 11. Each gateway allows the passage of a different quality of mental consciousness. These gateways act as filters allowing only mental consciousness carrying informing of a certain type through any particular gateway. The information carried by mental consciousness that appertains to human sexuality always passes through the lowest gateway from the mental body. It is the one that lies approximately in the area of the pubic bone. Human sexuality is a major area of preoccupation for the mind and the mental awareness that it generates is very deep, intense and powerful and it is intimately linked to location of the genital organs. Hence its passage through the gateway in the lower pelvic region. Awareness of issues that relate to your physical, emotional and material security pass through the gateway located between your pelvic bones. Mental consciousness carrying information relating directly to your sense of self or ego passes through your solar plexus gateway which is located a couple of inches below the lowest point of your breast bone. Being aware of your affection for another human being, animal or even the planet generates an intensity of mental consciousness that always emerges in to physical dimension through the gateway that is in the centre of your chest, near the location of the heart in your physical body. Consciousness generated by awareness concerning emotional expression and verbal communication passes through the gateway located in the neck or throat area. The mental consciousness generated by dwelling upon spiritual aspirations, God, the meaning of life and so on, generates a very subtle quality of mental consciousness that always passes through the so called the third eye, the highest gateway in the mental body. It lies just about one inch above the bridge of your nose. A side view of the location gateways is shown in figure 11 and a front view of the both gateways and structure of the mental body is shown in Figure 12.

CLEARING THE MENTAL BODY GATEWAYS

To ensure that consciousness has free passage from your mental to your physical body we suggest that you do the following exercise. Firstly, remind yourself of the exact location of the mental body gateways by referring to figures 10, 11.

Beginning with the uppermost gateway, think of it as a flower, any variety that seems appropriate, then imagine that particular kind of flower is floating in your third eye area. Imagine it as a closed bud. Look at its colour, shape and texture. Contemplate it deeply. Now in your minds eye see the flower bud beginning to grow and open spreading its petals wider and wider opening out to the light. Watch the flower until it is fully open. Allow your self to luxuriate in the experience of being this fully open flower open to the sun and sky of the physical world. Repeat this exercise for each of the rest of your mental body gateways working downwards. You will most probably find that the variety of flower you pick to represent a particular gateway changes, or that if the species is the same that the colour will be different. Simply go with whatever comes up in your mind.

The concept of some form of a vital life energy is pervasive within the basic understanding of the nature of life of virtually all ancient cultures. Each culture had its own name for this energy such as prana, ki or chi. As we said earlier in the chapter on the soul these kinds of energies are fundamentally related to the physical breath and its

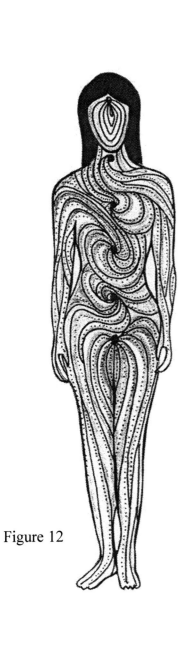

Figure 12

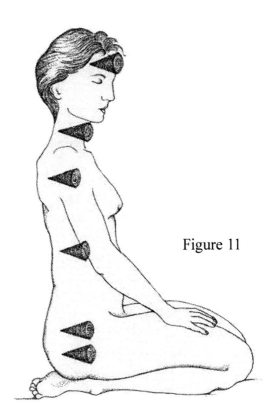

Figure 11

77

analogue in the mental body. The majority of the ancient healing practices within these cultures worked with these subtle breath energies and all the ways in which they could be influenced. These healing ancient processes and their more modern derivatives are basically working with the way in which the physical functioning of breath, blood and nervous system are mirrored in the mental body. Movement in the physical body is reflected in movement in the mental body. This movement is what we refer to as 'mind energy.' So mind energy can be understood to be the substance of the mental universe when it is in movement. Most of the modern so called 'energy' balancing techniques such as spiritual, psychic and magnetic healing, acupuncture and chakra balancing are in fact techniques that affect the moving mind stuff of the mental body, the mind energy, as well as the feed back loop of consciousness that exists from the physical body to the mental body and back to the physical body again. They are mind-body healing techniques. The effectiveness of these methods depends upon their ability to stimulate awareness in, and of, the mental body thereby activating the movement of the mind energy. They must also clear both the physical and mental body gateways so that consciousness can pass freely back and forth. What we would call soul-body healing is based upon techniques that work upon the feedback loop of consciousness between the soul and physical body. The ultimate in healing work is soul-body-mind healing and we are sure you can see what we mean by that term without any further explanation. To some extent any and all forms of healing could be called 'spiritual healing' in as much as they all stimulate the function of awareness to a greater or lesser degree.

Mind and emotion are the two dominant aspects of your being in the mental realm. In many teachings they are treated as two separate phenomena but this is an erroneous viewpoint. The two are inextricably linked, each being an aspect of the mental body. Therefore we do not speak of an emotional or astral body as it sometimes called as something separate and distinct from the mental body. Your mental body is both thought and emotion. In our exploration of these two phenomena we will begin with emotion as it arises first. We have already considered the nature of 'feelings' in our exploration of the soul. It is very important to be clear that feelings are not the same as the phenomenon commonly called 'emotions.' Emotions are an aspect of the mind. Specifically they are the sense of movement within your mental body. Remember that your mental body is created in the image of your physical body and we have already discussed the fact that the essence of the physical body is movement. So when physical consciousness flows into the mental realm much of the information that it carries appertains to the various kinds of movement within the physical body. That information is then structured into your mental body. Your mental body is not then a static form but a thought form that contains movement within it (Figure 12). Your perception or awareness of that movement when labelled by a particular word or thought is 'emotion.' For example, the sense of the mind stuff flowing upwards within your mental body accompanied by the word 'no' is the emotion of anger. Exactly the same movement within your mental body accompanied by the word 'yes' is the emotion of joy.

Lets think of a young girl child with a largely undeveloped mental body and follow the movement of consciousness within her. Awareness of movement within her soul body generates soul consciousness which carries this information to her physical body. When this soul consciousness impacts upon her physical body the information carried by it is structured into her physical body. Her awareness of the movement within her physical body is then a combination of the awareness of movement within her soul body coupled with the awareness of movement that is an intrinsic part of her physical body. Physical consciousness then carries this information, emanating from two different dimensions, to the mental realm where it becomes structured into her mental body. As much of the information is concerned with movement she begins to experience a very pure form of emotion, that is an emotion not coloured by any particular words. It is just the experience of movement within her mental body. Her emotions will be very fluid, changeable phenomena depending upon what is happening in the soul and physical parts of her being. To a great extent this is exactly how everyone's emotional life, if we may call it that, should be. So, very simply we can say that in your early life feelings and the consciousness generated by them ultimately form the basis of your emotions. It is only in later life that problems begin to arise as emotions are generated in relation to events that occur only within your mental world itself. Troublesome emotions nearly always arise independently of your soul and physical bodies.

The interesting thing about your emotions is that for most of the time they do not exist. What we mean by that is that unlike your physical body, your mental body is internally quite still most of the time. It only becomes active when it is being affected by some outside phenomena such as your perception of events in the physical world around you. Right now, at this very moment, as you read this paragraph are you aware of any emotion within you? No? Well we would have been very surprised if you were experiencing any. However, even though we said that emotion normally only appears in relation to some outside agent it can be triggered by activity taking place in your mental world itself. It does not have to be in the physical world at all. It could exist entirely in your own thoughts. If, as you are sitting reading this, you simply stop for a moment and imagine that someone is sitting opposite you just looking at you—where is this thought located ? Is it in your mental body or is it out beyond it somewhere in your own mental world? Now imagine that this same imaginary person is being verbally abusive to you in some way. Are you aware of movement in your mental body now, any stirring of emotion within you? Is the emotion you are experiencing as you listen to what they are saying one of anger? Did you perhaps experience some sense of movement in your mental body moving upwards from the centre of your mental body towards the head and shoulders? Were you aware of the words that were associated with this movement of mind stuff? Emotions can manifest in relation to either real or imaginary events. Please read that last sentence again because we can guarantee that with a little self observation you will discover that the majority of your emotional life occurs in relation to events that you only imagine happening in the mental dimension of your being not to real occurrences. You might also discover that you are spending a lot of time in certain emotional states that are rather less than enjoyable. You may also consider that it might be worth putting in some real work towards changing this situation if this is in any way true for you. It is obviously possible for you to learn to change your emotions by working directly with the movement of mind stuff in your mental body through your gift of awareness but it can also be done by looking at the words or thoughts that accompany the movement. So, let's look at the other aspect of your mental being which is mind.

Most of you will no doubt be familiar with the other form of activity in your mental being as thinking. We do not speak of mind as an object like your brain but as a process or activity. Thinking and the process that is mind are synonymous. Thinking is your processing of information. Information which, in your early life, is predominately carried into the mental plane of your being by your own physical consciousness. Though it must be said that the mental consciousness of your immediate family also has a role to play in this. However, in early life it is always easier for you to process your direct experience of your own physical consciousness. The process of thinking in the mental plane of existence is basically a phenomena of awareness. It is awareness that is active within different parts of your mental body, or it can be between some part of your mental body and a thought form or even a point of awareness that is located outside of it. It can even occur between different thought forms which exist outside of your mental body entirely. When awareness is active in two or more thought forms or places simultaneously, reflecting and re-reflecting consciousness back and forth, you are in the process of thinking. In general, most thinking takes place either within the confines and structure of your own mental body or between your mental body and a thought form outside it. The impact of the consciousness generated upon a thought form is an important factor in what you call creative thinking. Creative thinking basically involves processing information in some new and unique way. When awareness is active in two different forms reflecting consciousness back and forth the impact of that consciousness upon one or both of the thought forms will change the structure in some way, provided of course that the consciousness generated has sufficient energy. When this happens the information in the thought form has undergone some kind of transformation that may provide a new, valuable and creative insight into the area which the information in the thought form appertained to. On the other hand it may just be garbage! Ideally all thinking should be creative but often it is not and tends to be more of a re-inforcement of the existing thought form structures.

The act of thinking can be easily understood if it is looked at in terms of it being analogous to the functioning of your physical body. In your physical body various natural elements of the physical universe, which are combined in various complex forms or patterns, are taken in and processed or broken down into their constituent parts (digested) and then the fundamental elements are used to build or repair (assimilation) the structure of your physical body by being combined with it in different ways. Any waste materials from this process are eliminated (excretion) along with any other wastes from tissue repair and maintenance. The act of thinking in the mental realm is much the same. Your mental body takes in the basic element of the mental universe, mind stuff, which is combined in certain complex forms or patterns which you might call thoughts or ideas. These are digested or broken down into their fundamental patterns where their useful parts are assimilated and structured into your mental body or held nearby in other simple thought forms. Any waste mind stuff is eliminated or should be!

The source of food for your mental body is the free thought forms that are created by your own or someone else's mental processes. Awareness in your mental body generates mental consciousness which carries information back to the physical realm. Any mental consciousness that does not move directly into the physical universe but which radiates outward through your mental world attaches itself to the basic substance of the mental universe thereby patterning or encoding it. Such patterns or thought forms then being available to other people in the mental universe as food for their mental bodies—food for thought! These thought forms may also be stored away somewhere in your mental body or even outside of it to be a store of food for yourself at a later date, you could even think of them as mental fat stores if you like.

Whilst we are on the subject of food it is also true that physical and mental consciousness themselves are a food for the mental body. It is important to realise that when functioning well your mental body has an enormous appetite, far greater than that of your physical body in its universe. It is hungry for new thoughts, ideas, stimulation, experience and input generally. Its output of mental consciousness and new thought forms is just as great provided awareness is functioning fully. Here are a few questions you might like to consider. Is it spiral or circular thinking, when the same thought or thoughts repeat themselves endlessly within your awareness, eating your own mental regurgitated mental consciousness or to use an animal metaphor, endlessly chewing the cud? Does eating only your own mental consciousness plus the mind stuff it patterns, in other words your own thoughts and ideas constantly, mean being mentally stuck? What kind of mental diet do you eat? How good is your own mental body digestion? Does it have any parallels with your physical body's digestive process? Reflect on all that!

If, for example, you mindfully, thoughtfully with awareness, prepare a meal—a meal which in the physical universe might be composed of fruits and vegetables—you will also create for it a corresponding temporary mental body in your mental world which will also be food for the mental body of whoever consumes it. They will partake of both physical sustenance through its physical structure and their physical body as well as mental sustenance through the consumption of the mental body of the meal by their own mental body. The mental body of such a meal will perhaps be imbued with values such as respect and reverence for the source of the food. In which case it will a true ambrosia of the gods. On the other hand if it is prepared in haste and under pressure it is likely to be doubly indigestible.

The word 'mind' and terms like conscious mind, unconscious mind and even superconscious mind are in common usage in the modern world. Do you know what you mean by the word 'mind?' Do you always speak your mind? Do you know your own mind? Do you mind what other people think about you? Are you mindful of the consequences of your actions? Do you always bear the facts in mind? What's on your mind? You say that you don't really know, oh, well never mind! The word 'mind' and the word 'consciousness' are often used together in everyday language but what do they mean to you? What are they? Do you know what your unconscious mind is thinking? Can you swallow all this? There is more significance in these questions than simple word games and semantics.

Speaking of words, if we look at the familiar territory of your thoughts, in particular the thought processes that are synonymous with your internal dialogues or mind talk, we can see that thinking could also be said to involve you using words and relating them in different ways. A new and revolutionary idea could be said to be nothing more than a set of words combined in an unusual way. So what are 'words?' When as a child you are taught to speak, words are simply inner sounds that represent the physical consciousness you receive concerning external physical reality. Later, as you mature you learn other words that represent the consciousness of the inner physical reality of your bodily sensations, and still later you construct or learn more new words that represent the various processes and convolutions of your mental universe or world as a whole. Yet what is it that words actually represent?

If you see something as a child that you are told is a rose which happens to be red in colour and the following day you see another rose which is yellow how do you know that it is also a rose and is not in fact a daffodil? The answer to this is that the overall pattern of perception of the object matches that of the previous days experience of the red rose, though in many ways the yellow rose is quite different from the red rose. All roses are not alike but language, specifically the word rose, treats them as the same in spite of their differences.

The key in all this is the recognition of a pattern of experience or perception. Words are labels that you use to identify patterns of perception. Words represent thought patterns or forms, but unfortunately often only very broad categories of patterns, a fact that is of the utmost importance when using any technique that uses verbal constructs, such as an affirmation to modify your mental world in some way. Most people use words or language in such a way that one word is used to cover a large set of experiences or items. When this is the case you know that these people think in broad categories and react to situations on the basis of such generalisations. When this happens they can hardly be said to be experiencing the incredibly rich and varied range of experiences that life offers. Their reactions are nothing more than stereotyped patterns of response. There are cultures like the Polynesian who have literally dozens of words to describe different kinds of waves and clouds where most modern languages have but two or perhaps three at the most. The Eskimos have some twenty words describing different kinds of snow. Hopefully you can begin to see how responding to life only on the basis of simple word maps with their in-built limitations can make life an extremely drab, dull or even painful experience. Please don't say things in anger such as "all men (or women) are the same." The reality is that they are all quite different and unique in their own way. True, everyone one of them will be either a man or a woman but beyond that simple single word label they are all so different. Give yourself a chance to experience that difference. Study your usage of language and see how you use it to support or negate the richness and diversity of experience that being alive offers.

It is quite possible that you believe that thinking revolves entirely around the ability of the mind to use language. However, this kind of thinking is simply the one that you are made actively aware of every time that it is occurring. In fact, awareness is functioning at a low level between different parts of your mental body or between your mental body and other thought forms all the time. Sometimes this is a creative thinking process, sometimes not. What we are saying here is that awareness is not a uniform phenomenon. There are levels or degrees of awareness. For most of you the exercise of your awareness is going to be a fairly gross phenomenon, in as much as you will only be able to be aware of fairly high levels of activity in any particular body which generates large, though rather information poor, quantities of consciousness. To be able to perceive very subtle activation of spirit is a skill that you will have to learn over a long period of time through the practise of all the exercises that this book suggests. Spirit is active all the time but to a very limited degree. You could imagine it as a dark void in which, apart from the large points of light where awareness is very active, a totally random pattern of little sparks of light flicker and die in an unending dance. So, thinking is taking place throughout your mental realm at a level below your ability to perceive unless you actively seek it out through shining the light of your consciousness out into the darkness of your mental world to illuminate all the thought forms that exist within it.

To explore and come to know your mental-emotional self is very simple, it just requires an impartial self observation and therein lies the difficulty. Self observation is not too difficult a task but impartial self observation is another matter. We use the term impartial because your sense of self is in the mental realm. Your ego is very much who you would 'like' to believe yourself to be. It is not necessarily who you actually are.

For example, suppose a man who wants to explore his mind-self decides to write down the three most positive qualities that he thinks he has as a human being. He writes down that he is kind, honest and hard working. Now to exercise his power of self observation he decides to spend one whole day watching himself in action within his everyday life. Not evaluating, that will come later, but just observing. Now obviously, unless he is very skilled in keeping a point of awareness that is detached from the location of his mental body active all day, he is only going to have a partial picture of his behaviour but it will probably serve his purpose. At the end of the day, having gone to bed, he starts to review the day as best he can in the light of the three self perceptions that he wrote down. On reviewing his actions he sees that before going to work he kicked out in anger at his pet cat which was asking to be fed as he was eating his breakfast. Later he shouted abuse out of his car window at an elderly lady slowly crossing the road who held him up. Late for work, when questioned as to why by his employer, he said it was the traffic and yet in reality he had overslept after a late night. Later on he blamed a colleague for the late completion of a sales report that he himself had mislaid. After lunch he told his secretary that he had an important meeting with a new client and yet in fact he just went to the golf course. Are these actions those of a kind, honest, hard working person? Of course not. But can he see this? Now the very 'partial' self justification can begin. His boss often takes an afternoon off so why shouldn't he? The elderly lady made him late for work so he was justified in shouting at her. It made her move more quickly anyway. The cat should realise he isn't at his best first thing in the morning and so on. You might like to try a similar exercise yourself. The self observation part is relatively easy. It is the impartial evaluation that is so difficult. Your image of your self is mostly what you wish to believe yourself to be not what you are. You all create mental realities or worlds that will support those cherished self perceptions that you hold, but do they resemble reality in any way? If you wish to discover the nature of the emotional aspect of your mind self, impartial self observation is the key. Study your emotional responses in your everyday life. It's just as simple, or as difficult, as that. See if you can discover the key to being impartial and objective in relation to your self.

You are all so powerful in the mental universe that you can construct your mental world to suit any criteria. In the mental realm you all live in different worlds. You can construct a mental world in which a few innocuous words from a stranger are, in your mental reality, a deadly insult, or that the caring support of a partner is to you a suffocating, restricting pressure. Perhaps the idea that you all live in different mental worlds needs some exploration.

Superficially, it seems to be stupid to say that you all live in different worlds. After all the world you live in is the same as the world your next door neighbour lives in, or is it? If you think about it, is your perception of the nature of the world that you live in the same as everyone else? You probably assume that it is, but is that actually true? Surely you have tried to explain to someone the colour of an object by using a verbal description and found that you had to resort to pointing out some other object around you of similar colour to get the information across, only to then have them protest that the colour you were trying to describe sounded nothing like the colour of the object that you pointed out as an example. You assume that when you use the same words as other people that they mean the same thing to all of you. The reality is that in the great majority of cases they do not. If this is true of your verbal maps or models of reality, and as words are the major way in which you communicate about your own mental world with other people, do you begin to see how difficult it is to really to communicate with another person?

The world that each individual lives in is a construct based on their early perceptual experience of the physical world and how the people around them told them to label the internal experiences that they had in response to it. Further complications arise as a child tries to refine its understanding of the world around it through the difficulties encountered in trying to express and communicate the complex patterns of perception that it has with a very limited vocabulary. Your sense of reality, the world that you live in, is strongly influenced by the particular culture that you grow up in. The overall consensus of opinion, as held by the people who make up that culture, on the nature of reality is of enormous power in structuring your perceptions of life. The historical milieu that you live in is also of great importance in determining your understanding of the nature of the world that you inhabit. If you study your own experience, and in particular the times when you were really totally unable to get a clear understanding of another person's point of view, does it not clarify things if you assume that you were both talking about two different worlds and that the nature of the world that they were trying to share with you was not part of your experience in any way. In fact, if you could have had that realisation at the time would you not have been able to gracefully admit the validity of their opinion concerning the functioning of their unique world without feeling in any way threatened by that difference? Then perhaps you would not have needed to support the existence of your world by proving their world to be false.

It is important to realise that all personal perceptions of reality are valid. They all work for the people who have them. That you might find them difficult to understand or to live in may well be true, but that does not invalidate them in any way. The truth is that all your worlds are very real to each of you and that the mental universe is able to support an infinite number of different realities within it. Indeed, as many different realities or personal worlds as there are minds to create them. Do you think that the world of the lowly house fly in your kitchen is the same as the world you live in? It is not, and this is because the fly's perceptual organs are totally different. Its sense of time is totally different which is why it is so hard to swat a fly because what to you is a really fast hand movement, to the fly is a slow motion strike. It can easily avoid the strike at what appears to you to be the last moment but which to the fly is long before the strike would have landed. The fly's mental universe, its visual model of the world, is quite different from your own. Its perception of the structure of the kitchen, the actual look of it is totally different. This all occurs because the fly's organs of perception are structurally different to those of a human being. However, the fly's interpretation of its experience of the world is governed for all flies by instinct, by previously established patterns of processing in its mental universe and because this is so we can postulate that all flies live in the same physical and mental worlds. They all experience the world in exactly the same way. It looks, smells and feels the same to all of them. This fact certainly helps communication between them! Whereas, your interpretation, your self reflections concerning information that you receive via your senses is a learned skill which is influenced by an infinite number of factors. In a way, you might think that it is a shame that you no longer have an instinctual skill like that of the fly, and indeed most other animals, in interpreting the patterns of sensation that occur through your sense organs. Many wars have been fought over one nation trying to convince another concerning the absolute validity of its particular view of the world. However, if this was the case you would not have the ability of self transcendence because you would have sacrificed the possibilities of an individual mind that can create its own unique mental reality for a fully developed 'group' mind that has only one model of the universe. You would loose out on all the enormous variety that life offers because you would be pre-programmed, so to speak, to only respond to events in certain ways. A relatively safe existence perhaps but potentially very dull.

One of the single most important facts to be grasped concerning the domain of the mind is that you create everything in your mental life. You are creator of your mental world. When we say this we do not mean that you create the basic element of the mental universe, 'mind stuff,' but that you take it and mould it into your interpretation of the information you receive from your physical body via consciousness. Initially the creation of your mental world is strongly influenced by your parents and other adults in your early life. They give you information concerning its basic construction techniques. Though once you have mastered the basic skills your mental world becomes very much your creation. Having created it you are then responsible for running it. Your perception of its overall shape and structure and all that you have created within it, are your responsibility. You are also responsible for the dynamic interactions between the various different parts of it.

The problem all human beings face, with full control over their mental worlds, can be illustrated by thinking of it as an automobile you created out of simple raw materials but without any real first hand experience in its design and function. Having built it you started it running, but just as it began to move you fell asleep because building a car is very tiring. Unfortunately, you also let go of the steering wheel so the car continues on its path totally out of control and going who knows where. Even if you wake up, you realise you do not know how to control it properly because you did not learn how through simple experiments designed to explore its capabilities. You did no proper test or trial runs. Even if you did, on some brief test runs things probably got pretty scary, so you stopped long before you learned how to control the power available to you. A great deal of time and energy needs to be expended before you can finally be said to have mastered the art of driving your car. Indeed, sometimes, in the process of your testing you may well discover that your design is fundamentally defective. You have created a car that can never be driven safely. You may well need to rethink your whole concept of what a car actually is and what it should be able to do!

We wonder if you now realise that because your mental world is so powerful it can, and frequently does, dominate your understanding and perception of reality. Often to the extent that you mistake your mental world for the physical world. We can say with authority that few of you actually know what the real physical universe is like. Many of your scientists are caught in this trap trying to do experiments to discover the laws that govern the reality of a physical universe that does not exist outside their own minds. A reality which is really only an interpretation of the true physical universe. This being the case sometimes they get it right and sometimes they get it disastrously wrong. As long as the gateway is clear physical consciousness faithfully carries information concerning the physical universe into your mental realm, but after a certain point in your life it is you, your mental self, with all your attitudes and opinions that interpret that consciousness and fit it into some kind of construct in your mental world. Provided your mental world does not dominate your existence and if your mental consciousness feeds information concerning the mental constructs that you have created representing the physical world back to your physical body, your body self will respond sending new physical consciousness back to your mind, containing information relating to the accuracy of your mental constructs. This feedback loop and its continuing function becomes the mechanism by which you can refine the pattern and shape of your mental world until it is a true and accurate representation of the physical world. However, you must try and experience physical consciousness without filtering it through other thought forms or beliefs.

It is vitally important to realise that the second biggest misuse of your mind, after that of allowing it to dominate the whole of your being, is to allow it to develop patterns that give survival value to the things in your lives that could at most be described as wants, likes or desires. It could be said that the body self serves the Life principle, the mind self serves the Love principle and the soul-self the God principle. To experience love from your environment is not a survival issue although in most peoples minds it seems that they believe it is. They act as if whether or not they are loved by another person in their life is a matter of life and death. Virtually all the craziness that surrounds relationships stems from this life or death attitude. You do not need love from another because all the love you ever need is already there within you, in the form of the absolutely unconditional love that your own soul or higher self offers—its soul consciousness. It is also true that many people make success and fame into survival issues and into patterns held in their mind that constantly make their interaction with others in the work arena a matter of life and death. They become both obsessed and possessed by things that are of little or no real importance in terms of their continuing life on earth.

To be able to disentangle that life or death attitude, that sense of utter and deadly seriousness concerning the issues in your mental reality, around which you have woven them, is no easy task. The first thing you have to do is identify which things in your life you treat as life or death issues that, in reality, have no such intrinsic survival value. You might think that many things in your life really do have that much importance but ask yourself what the true survival needs of a human being are. List them all. Write them down if it helps. What are the things which you cannot survive without. We can hear some of you saying that having money is a survival issue because it can buy all the things that the body needs, but the operative word in that thought is 'can.' All the things that money can buy that support your physical life can also be obtained without having money through barter for example. So, is it really a survival issue? In reality most survival issues revolve around the body. Physical survival requires the presence of soul consciousness, food and water as well some form of shelter to provide warmth and periods of rest. Mental survival requires one very simple thing and that is input, or information, which is provided by physical and mental consciousness. Indeed, if you do not provide that input it will often try and create its own through hallucination. Soul survival just requires the presence of the original spark of divine consciousness that created the soul body to continue to exist.

In the light of these comments on the requirements for human survival analyse each area on your list in detail. Eliminate all the areas that are not of absolute importance to your continuing survival. Once you have your list honed right down to the essentials, study it and allow yourself to realise that these are your only true *needs*. Anything else apart from that which you have on your list are just things that you would like to experience. To have any of them will not make your chances of survival greater in the slightest degree. If you are still having difficulty sorting out your needs from your wants then try asking yourself this "If I was told that I only had two or three months to live would I worry about obtaining this in my life?" The presence of death, as a fundamental part of life, is a great teacher. To contemplate deeply on the absolute certainty of your own death is an excellent way to cut through all your life and death bullshit.

Always try and have a sense of proportion concerning the things in your life that you think that you need. Periodically ask your self the question when you find yourself getting deadly serious about some issue. "If I had this would it make my survival more certain?" We can almost guarantee you that whatever it is, it's not that important. Lighten up. Let a little more soul consciousness shine through. The power of Love has the power to dispel the clouds of darkness that accompany such moments but for this to happen don't think, just *feel*.

As human beings you have the ability to control your mental processes, your thinking, particularly your internal mind talk. You also have the ability to change your usage of language which can have far reaching implications. Changing your usage of words or using them with an understanding of the limitations inherent in the way language categorises experience can open up an enormous range of new reactions and life experiences for you. The fact that you can control your thinking means that you can control your whole mental universe, its construction, your perception of it and your responses to it. It is in this sense that it can be said that you do actually create your life, specifically your mental life which for many of you is your whole life, due to the dominance of your mind over the rest of your being. If you doubt that your thinking and perception is pattern based, as well as being a learned skill, and that it can shape your experience so drastically, a look at people born blind who in later life, perhaps through medical treatment, are enabled to see is definitely instructive. What has happened is that as soon as they were able to see, the information passed into their mental realm seemed meaningless to them. Just a chaos of patterns. In other words they did not automatically see as you might see, not things recognisable as faces, trees or houses but jumbled patterns of light rather like you might experience the visual effect of a kaleidoscope. They had to be taught how to interpret the patterns of information. In other words perception itself is not a passive phenomena. It is an active process in which information carried by physical consciousness into the mental dimension is made sense of on the basis of learned ways of sorting and organising. Perception then is fully under your control. Your perceptions are your responsibility. You can alter them and it is within your power to do so. Taking all this into account we can say that in the mental realm your perceptions, your reactions to your perceptions, and your actions based upon your reactions to your perceptions are all under your control. You create it all and so you can also recreate it all in any form you desire. You can create it to serve the Love principle, to bring joy and happiness into manifestation within your being or you can create it in such a way that pain and suffering are your lot in life.

You have much food for thought in this chapter. The challenge is to achieve total mastery of your mental world. This is often easier said than done but in essence you begin by simply watching your mind and allowing your awareness of it to be as complete as possible. See if you can discover the laws by which your own unique mental world is governed. As you penetrate into the complexities of it, know that you yourself created it the way it is and that perhaps some of it was given to you that way, as fact, but that too was, in the first instance, created by someone. Remind yourself that if it was created by a human being, you or others, it can also be changed by you. Begin to create the kind of mental world that you would like to live in. Perhaps even a world governed by Love and your own soul. The actual techniques for changing your world are many and varied. Indeed, many of the other techniques offered in this book can be adapted to help you change your mind. The process of change itself can bring up some interesting issues, some of which we will explore next, as well as offering a specific method of creating change and giving you greater choice in your mental world.

CHAPTER 5

CHANGE

When we looked at consciousness itself we said that it had both radiance and impact as well as being an information carrier. In looking at the process of change we will consider in more depth this aspect of the impact of consciousness. We have already said that soul consciousness is like fire and one of the effects of that fire is to heat the soul body. One of the other effects of heating any object, like say a piece of metal, is that as it gets hotter it expands. As soul consciousness impacts directly upon the physical body it does not heat it up per se but it does create an expansion. Indeed we have already looked at this effect in our exploration of the physical body, specifically in relation to the exercise on walking in the presence of love. Physical consciousness which we likened to water has a lubricating effect upon the physical body in that it creates an ease and fluidity of movement between all the organs and muscles. An effect that is essential to your physical health. The next question to ask is what is the impact of physical consciousness upon the mental and soul bodies.

Well, one of the other qualities of water that we mentioned was that it dissolves things and it is just that quality which effects the mental body. It helps to break down fixed structures in the mental body and combat rigid thinking. The impact of physical consciousness on the soul body is to literally cool down or balance the fiery enthusiasm that can envelope and suffuse the soul body. Thus creating a more appropriate resonance between the needs of the soul and the facts concerning events in physical reality.

When we looked at mental consciousness we described how it filled up the mental body. We also spoke of air as a having a quality of movement which is exactly its effect on the physical body. It initiates physical movement predominately in terms of the muscle structure and the translation of the whole of the body through physical space. Problems arise due to the fragmentary nature of mental consciousness in that up to six slightly different qualities of mental consciousness can impact upon the physical body at any one time, all of which can trigger movement and sometimes the directions of that movement are quite different, which creates all sorts of conflict within the body self.

As consciousness is also a radiant phenomena we should also consider its impact upon other people. We have already described how any particular quality of consciousness that you generate does not just pass information from one dimension of your being to another but also radiates outward through the particular realm in which it was generated. Your radiating mental consciousness has the same impact upon someone else's mental body as it does on your own. It fills it up. When you radiate soul consciousness it will heat up any other soul bodies upon whom it impacts and when you generate physical consciousness it will literally lubricate or make more fluid the physical bodies of any one whom it strikes. It is also absolutely important to be aware that perhaps the one primary effect of radiating consciousness, whatever its nature, upon other people is its effect upon spirit. It makes it active.

Radiating consciousness generates awareness which, of course, in turn generates more consciousness. It is also important to remember that the final aspect of the impact of consciousness is not in its direct effect upon the three bodies or spirit but in the impact of the actual information that it carries upon the self in each realm.

So, to summarise. Just as ordinary light in the physical realm exerts pressure so does the light of consciousness. Consciousness of whatever quality has impact. It can literally move you in some way. That movement creates an internal change in your position, a change in your awareness. Any change in your awareness alters your sense of self. Your self-reflections are different. You perceive yourself to be different. You view yourself from a different perspective. When someone expresses a thought to you, from their mental realm through the medium of their voice, it is easy to tell if that thought is part of their being, a part of their self-understanding, because if it is it will have a direct impact on you. It will move you in some way. You are not moved by just the words but predominately by the consciousness that accompanies them. The mental consciousness that accompanies the verbal expression of an idea that is a part of a person's 'beingness,' their self understanding, their self-reflection carries the same information. It is that consciousness whose message is the same as the words that the other person is speaking that grips you, enthralls you and changes you.

Lets look at the process of change in a very general sense first and see what we can learn about it before looking at the process very specifically in relation to the human being. To begin, imagine that you have just built your own new home which, as it happens, is a log cabin. Within a couple of months of you completing it and moving in, a hurricane force storm hits the area and the house is literally razed to the ground. Your only recourse is to completely rebuild the house but, of course, this time you will build it much stronger in case another storm should strike. You will probably use deeper foundations as well as thicker walls and better internal bracing. This scenario is quite a traumatic experience on all levels. However, suppose we change the story a little and have only a gale force storm hit the house. Now in this case you will probably be aware that the house is moving in the high winds, which tells you instantly that you must strengthen the structure in some way. The cabin may even sustain some structural damage but you know that can be repaired after the gale has passed. In all, a far less traumatic experience, mainly due to the fact that the intensity of the external stimulus affecting the cabin was much less. The pain involved both physically and emotionally in the first situation is far greater than that in the second. In each case the response is ultimately the same—the need to strengthen the structure of the cabin.

In general terms then, any object should have sufficient structural integrity, such that should it be put under stress, it will be both stable and strong enough to deal with that stress without damage. If it is not then a deformation of its structure will result. In some cases it may collapse entirely when placed under the stress or simply deform until it is no longer able to perform its intended function properly. Any deformation of a structure is a destructive process and in a human being any such process is characterised by the experience of pain. The greater the deformation, the greater the pain. This deformation is itself a process of change and pain can be an intrinsic part of the process. What determines the degree of change is the intensity or strength of the initial stimulus and the duration for which it is applied.

Obviously a fairly weak force applied over a long period of time can be as destructive as a very powerful one applied for a brief instant. In the case of weak force acting over a long period, it is possible to modify the structure to meet that force without too much disruption to the function of the structure and with minimum structural change. In human terms such a situation would not create any great experience of pain. However, in the case of a very strong force acting over a short period of time the whole structure could collapse, or at the very least suffer severe damage making it impossible for it to fulfil its intended function. This would necessitate massive reconstruction and modification, not simply the rebuilding of a duplicate structure. This situation in a human being would be characterised by a huge amount of pain.

When looking at the process of change in relation to the soul the first thing to be clear about is that the soul body and higher self are the most flexible, resilient aspects of a human being. The soul body is a form held together by the attractive effect of the soul pattern upon the free unbound life energy in its dimension of existence. It is not a rigid structure and is therefore not subject to stress in the same way as the rigid structure in our last example. Also, time does not exist in relation to the soul therefore the concept of the rate at which changes occurs is not relevant in any way. This is not to say that the soul is not subject to stress, because it is. The most fundamental form that it takes is when the soul cannot express itself freely. This occurs when a person has no awareness of their soul so neither listens to it nor allows it to have any impact on their life, by living almost exclusively in the mental realm. In this case you could speak of the higher self as experiencing a form of frustration which would change the structure of the soul body in that it would begin to contract and collapse, occupying less space than would be normal. Change in the soul body and higher self is an instantaneous phenomenon that happens naturally as soon as you allow yourself to be aware of its existence, and allow its soul consciousness to have impact in your life again.

You can see more clearly the relevance of our exploration of the process of change in general terms when looking at the physical body. Change in the physical body does occur due to an external stimulus of some kind. The major change that occurs in the physical body is growth. In particular growth of muscle tissue. This only happens in relation to a stimulus and in this case the most common stimulus is repeated movement over a period of time. In everyday language, we are of course referring to exercise. If we look at the actual physical response to exercise we can see the specific application of the general concepts of change that we developed above. When you exercise, muscle tissue is actually torn down and destroyed due to the demands of the movement you are performing. The body then has to replace that damaged tissue but it does not replace it exactly as it was before because obviously it was inadequate to the demands placed upon it by the exercise. So, the body replaces it with more muscle tissue but in greater quantity. Thereby making it more capable of meeting the demands of the stimulus that is placed upon it. There is one thing that characterises this whole process and that is the sensation of soreness or pain experienced within about a day of finishing the exercise in question. It is possible to control the pain experienced through the changes exercise brings about by shortening the time for which we exercise or by doing only gentle forms of exercise. Which is of course fully in keeping with the general principles we derived earlier.

It is important to be aware that ordinary repair processes in the body do not actually constitute a process of change, because what you are looking at is cellular replication.

The structure in question is simply replaced without any change or alteration to its basic architecture or function. A damaged cell of liver tissue is replaced by another similar cell and not say, a brain cell. If that actually happened we are talking about a real change, potentially a very destructive one, but ordinary cellular repair involves simple duplication not change.

However, the process of repair or healing in the body is something we should consider further because the need for that repair often, though not always, is caused by the effect of an external stimulus upon the body which could range from, for example, a bacteriological or viral infection to a physical blow. If, for arguments sake, you have a bronchial infection caused by a particular bacterial agent that is destroying the cellular structure of your lungs, your own body cannot repair the damaged cells because the outside force i.e. the bacteria, is constantly stressing the whole structure thereby making it impossible for reconstruction or healing to occur. In this case you do need a change, otherwise you will not recover from the infection. In most cases the change will come about either through the body's immune system destroying the infection, or through taking a course of antibiotic drugs which effectively eliminates the stress upon the structure of the lungs so that healing can occur. The change we are talking about here is from a condition in which cellular reconstruction can not happen to one in which it can. The key factor in this situation is the removal of the outside stimulus that prevents normal healing rather than the need to change or strengthen the body's innate ability to repair or replace damaged tissue. Of course, it could also be said in this kind of situation that the function of the immune system itself is in need of changing if it can not deal with the infection quickly and efficiently. In this case you are looking at a structure or bodily system that cannot fulfil its function when stressed externally. The solutions that present themselves are essentially very simple either you remove the external stimulus through a change of environment, appropriate alternative or allopathic medical therapy, which might even include surgery, or we strengthen the basic structure. We could and perhaps should consider seriously how to do both simultaneously.

How do you strengthen the structure of the immune system? Firstly, you must make sure that there is more than adequate nutrition which will provide the basic building blocks for the new reconstructed immune system. Secondly, you must deal with the impact of mental consciousness upon the body. We have already pointed out that the effect of mental consciousness on the physical body is to create movement through the muscle structure but it also creates movement right down to the cellular level. In particular the movement of blood and lymph. Going back to our example of a bronchial infection, if there is a quality of mental consciousness emanating from the gateway in the chest area which creates a subtle movement of tissue fluid in the lungs away from the focus of the infection, then it is going to be very difficult for the body to get the cells which fight infection to the area where they are needed. Alternatively, if there is no mental consciousness passing through the gateway in the chest then there is no positive support for the physical movement of the cells of the immune system to get to the site of infection. Cells will get there but perhaps not in as great a number or as quickly as desirable. Thirdly, there is often a need to change a person's outer environment in some way. Remember that another person's mental consciousness can have an impact, possibly an undesirable one. Particularly if you are close to the person in question and it is someone who shares your mental reality.

You have surely heard of people who have an almost suffocating effect on the people around them. Sometimes the planetary consciousness itself in a particular location can have an inhibiting effect upon immune system function. In which case it is desirable to move physically to another area. Then there is the need to investigate the person's lifestyle in general. Their occupation and leisure pursuits need to be explored to see what impact they are having both physically and mentally. We know also that soul expression could also be a vital factor to explore and we refer you back to the exercise on walking in the presence of love in which we explored in detail the positive effect of soul consciousness on the functioning of the physical body. In simple terms the basic need is to remove all the inhibiting stresses in a person's life both mentally and physically as well as reconnecting them to the reality of their soul.

We should examine this whole concept of planetary influence in a little more detail before continuing with our exploration of change. Man does not exist separately from the Earth and the rest of the solar system. The consciousness that emanates from these great beings can have a profound affect upon your life. For most of you the degree of harmony between your aims and aspirations and that of the planets is at best a random event. Sometimes they are aligned and at other times they are in total and frustrating opposition. However, it is possible to gain a perception of the influence on your life of the other great bodies of consciousness in the solar system, namely of course the sun and all the other planets. This subject can be explored pragmatically and theoretically through a study of the science of astrology but it can also be experienced at a feeling level during a soul body gateway clearance, as described earlier in this book. This can be done by simply expanding your awareness to embrace what you conceive any particular one of the planets to be like and then allowing your higher self to fill in the details of its action upon you.

The understanding of the interaction of the planet in question and your own life may come to you as thoughts, images or emotions during the experience. Any book on the solar system will give you sufficient basic information concerning the planets to enable your mind to tune in appropriately. If you can deepen your perception of the consciousness of the planets as they act in your life it becomes a natural process to work in harmony with these incredibly powerful entities. Do not forget that the Earth itself is alive and generates huge amounts of consciousness that have a profound impact on your life. Quite often it is not the other planets in the solar system that are resisting your attempts to change but the Earth itself. It is a simple matter to adapt the above exercise so as to ascertain the nature of the interaction between your self and the Earth.

If movement and change is virtually an inescapable process in the physical body, and if movement is life, then in terms of their ego or mind-self responses to life most people are already dead. When was the last time you changed your mind? How fluid are your attitudes? When was the last time you changed one of your beliefs about life? How are you going to deal with all the undoubtedly new concepts and different ways of perceiving reality that this book offers? Is your mind and mental self sufficiently flexible and alive to cope with the complexities of life? The answer to this last question is, for the great majority of people, "No."

When you think of the concept of 'change,' in particular changing your mind, or your self, you probably see it as the need to stop doing something and to substitute something better or more effective in its place. However, this concept of the process of change is inevitably going to bring up a fear of loss within you because you will no longer be the same if you give something up. You will no longer know your self and this situation will be perceived in some part of your being as a kind of psychic death. A death of the mind-self or ego. All death engenders feelings of grief and loss as well as creating a desire to bring the departed back again. These feelings create a fundamental resistance to the whole idea of change, which is why it is so difficult for most people to achieve. To make the process of change easy you need an understanding of it in which it is perceived as a gain not a loss. If you see change as a learning process you will find the whole thing a much simpler matter. Change in the mental realm is a process in which you learn or enable different responses to recurrent situations in your life. Ideally these different responses will be founded upon new feelings about, and new perceptions of your self. This understanding of change will allow you to view it as an enjoyable process. It will feel like an expansion and growth of your being not a death. It will be facilitating the life principle.

Many of you will no doubt in the past have experienced pain in relation to the phenomena of change in your lives. Change, whether self initiated or visited upon you from without can, as we discussed earlier in our look at some general principles of change, be very painful when the rate at which you or your life are changing exceeds your ability to handle it easily. Integrating the impact of change and its significance into your perception of your self and your life as a whole can be a complicated and difficult process. This pain that you all experience when the rate at which you are changing exceeds your ability to cope comfortably, forms yet another resistance to change. To avoid this phenomena you need to study in some detail the process of change as it has arisen during the past in your own life so that you can ascertain those changes that you found easy to integrate and those that you did not. It should be quite easy to discover which changes in the past have been a problem for you. Now, what about the rate at which they happened ? Do you think that some of them would perhaps have been easier, even pain free, if they had occurred at a slower pace. Explore, in your mind's eye, a particular painful scenario from your past, as it actually happened. See it as if watching a movie. Notice how you felt throughout the experience then try running the same scenario again from the beginning but slow the whole process down. Notice if that makes a difference to your emotions and feelings. Is it as painful as before? If you continue slowing down the process can you tell when you reach the rate at below which no actual change would be taking place.

The pain you feel in relation to mental change is quite often your resistance to that change, not in fact the experience of a mental structure or pattern collapsing or being reconstructed. A reduction in the rate of change reduces the pain because you can relax and feel that you do not have to resist it so strongly. This pain or resistance is directly related to your need to be in control of your existence. The opposite stance to resisting change and being in control of your life is to view life as a mystery adventure and the changes in it as the unfolding of the story. A life lived in anticipation of the changes as opposed to a life lived in fear of the changes.

Of course this is easier said than done. Many of you will have built elaborate structures in your lives which you will be very loathe to see altered. However, have you noticed how just when you think that everything is under control and that you have your life going just as you want it, that some externally generated event has an unpleasant habit of coming along and knocking your carefully constructed life flat on its face. In reality, trying to create a life that has the minimum of change within it is to create a structure that is not in any way part of the great universal process of change that is life. The great immune system of reality itself will almost automatically be drawn to such anti-life structures and will begin to try and breath life into them by breaking them up, creating movement and change within them.

It would be valuable for you to look at your own life and any control structures that you use to maintain it to ascertain just how attached you are to your world in its present form. The more attached you are the greater the pain is going to be when the inevitable change comes. This is not to say that you should always rush out to meet change with open arms. There must be periods of time for consolidation and integration after the impact of any major reformation. These time periods are different for everybody and vary according to the nature of the change. Be gentle with yourself. Don't rush things. Life itself will show you when things need to be done quickly by creating rapid external change. When seeking to change yourself be aware of your resistance, do not try to push things, take your time, be easy on yourself. However, do not talk yourself into stagnation under the guise of taking great good care of your self. To help you to heal your understanding of change it is possible to modify the technique from the chapter on the body in which you enfold a specific body part with love. All you need to do is symbolise, in some form, your current attitude towards change. Then apply the heat of your soul consciousness to it by joining that image with the symbol of love that arises in your thoughts.

It is almost certainly true that the things about yourself that you would like to change are both useful and valid behaviours or responses in some circumstances. The reality is that you probably over use them. You try and make a certain behaviour or response work in all the life situations that you meet rather than using it selectively. Whilst change can be seen as a learning process, it can also be described as a process of non-action, in as much as by not allowing yourself to fall into an old pattern of reaction new responses will arise spontaneously from your being.

With this in mind, change becomes a fairly simple matter of just inhibiting your old responses. To change effectively it is not necessary to try and foresee what the most appropriate response to a certain situation might be and then try and learn how to implement it. What is important is not thinking or reacting in an old pattern. In actual fact you will discover that you have already learned numerous other responses to any particular situation. When you inhibit your old reactions a selection of the most appropriate of these other possibilities will always arise in your mind from which you can then chose how you are going to respond. Indeed, if you allow yourself to perceive change as a process of 'not doing' rather than doing you will also avoid rousing any feelings of inadequacy that you may have around your learning capabilities which could possibly form yet another resistance to change.

It may seem to you that the idea that change is very easy to achieve is a preposterous statement, particularly if you have tried to change in the past and failed. Often the difficulty lies in the fact that few people realise that their responses to situations are in actual fact based on accessing in some part of their minds a long series of detailed thoughts that follow their own particular logic. You do not realise that this is what happens because it all takes place so fast, in practical terms within perhaps an eighth of a second or even less. The fact that it all happens so fast can lead you to believe that you simply respond to a situation without any thought, deliberation or choice of any kind. You can also end up feeling doomed and at the mercy of your personality, not realising that it was you who created your responses in the first place and that therefore you can change them. It is your sheer familiarity with certain trains of thought, that allow you to react so fast. This familiarity and a concurrent increase in your speed of reaction grows as you repeatedly apply a particular pattern of thinking to a situation whenever it arises in your life. Just to prove that this is, in actual fact, what you do just try the following exercise.

FREEZE FRAME FOR CHANGE

Firstly choose a particular habitual response that you have to a recurrent situation. This could be anything. It could be how you respond when someone shouts at you, or how you respond to a perceived social injustice, or your response when something that you or someone else has done does not match up to what your earlier expectation of the final outcome was going to be. Having selected the habitual response that you want to examine, sit or lie down on a comfortable position and take a deep breath, expelling the air in roughly three equal parts. Repeat this process three times.

Now, allow yourself to remember the most recent time you experienced the situation that draws the response to be analysed. See the situation and the response in your mind's eye. See it like a movie on a cinema screen. We are sure that you are aware that a film is actually composed of many single images each showing the action as it occurred in a small fragment of time. When these images are projected quickly one after the other on the screen they give the sense of ordinary movement and activity. At some time you may have even been in a cinema when for some reason the projector accidentally slowed down and you saw the action projected in slow motion, one step at a time. We want you to do exactly the same thing with the short film that you now have in your mind's eye concerning the situation that you are exploring. You need to slow your film down until you literally see it happening one frame at a time and advancing at the rate of one frame every five seconds or perhaps even slower.

What is unique about your film is that with each individual frame you can experience any thoughts or physical sensations that are happening to you in your film at that moment without distortion. Now simply watch the whole of your film noting how you feel at each particular step of the way. Having completed this exercise we are sure that you now realise just how many different thoughts and feelings occur in your habitual response to any particular situation.

As a simple example suppose your film concerns your habitually angry response to anyone who criticises something that you are doing. As you slow your film down, in the first frame you hear their criticism. In the second frame you hear yourself thinking, "Oh, they are criticising me." In the third frame you are thinking, "They are angry with me." In the fourth frame you are thinking, "I don't think that there was anything wrong with what I did." In the fifth frame you hear yourself thinking, "I did not do it to upset them." and you feel your physical body collapsing as if you have been wounded. In the six frame you feel your body tensing up and hear yourself thinking "Why should I listen to them. They obviously don't like me." In the seventh frame you are thinking, "What right do they have to criticise me." In the eighth frame you feel your face getting hot and you are thinking, "They are the one with the problem, not me." Then, in the ninth frame you actually hear yourself shouting very angrily at them "Rubbish, How dare you criticise me! I am totally justified in what I did."

As you can see there are a number of thoughts and feelings that go to make up the habitual response in this example. You will also notice that there was a sudden shift between the fifth and sixth frames. Up to the fifth frame the thoughts were of a fairly calm, analytical nature simply looking at the facts of the experience in detail. However, by the sixth frame you have, in a sense, decided that the criticism was unjustified, that you had no intention of creating a problem for the other person and in fact feel hurt by the fact that they do not seem to realise that. So, you then go on the offensive because hurt people often hurt back or to use another phrase, "the best defence of yourself is a good offense." To change your response in this example the main thing you would need to do is prevent your response from getting beyond frame four because up to this point all your responses are simple calm objective thoughts concerning the situation. After this point a number of thoughts and powerful emotions are evoked which would be useful to avoid. As we said earlier all you need to do is inhibit your old response to any situation so as to allow for new ones to arise. Effectively seeking spontaneous change through non-action rather than trying to substitute new behaviours over the top of old.

Having actually ascertained that all your seemingly instantaneous responses to situations are in fact built up of a great number of different elements that occur extremely quickly the simplest way to inhibit them is to implant an automatic freeze frame or pause in your mind in relation to any particular response that you would like to change. A freeze frame in your mental realm allows soul and physical level responses to arise easily without interference. To implant a pause or freeze frame is actually very easy and follows on from your frame by frame analysis of the response in question. Run the same film that you have been working with in your mind's eye once more, but this time you need to expand your visual field to take in the projector. Make sure, as you focus on the projector, that you can see the freeze frame or pause switch or button. Now watch the film once more in slow motion up to the point at which you would like to stop the action. The point before any negative or old repetitive actions or thoughts occur. As soon as you reach the frame before that point see yourself pressing the pause button. Look at the screen and notice that the film has stopped at the point that you wanted it to. Notice how you feel. Now, see yourself pressing another button beside the freeze frame marked 'auto-repeat.' This will ensure that the stop always occurs at this point in this particular kind of scenario. The freeze frame is now programmed into the projection system. At this point, rewind the film and run it again to make sure that you have programmed the pause in at the right place and that it is working properly. If it doesn't, just repeat these steps until it does work perfectly. You might find it necessary to modify the pause and automatic repeat sequence to better suit your own idea of how it should be done before the system is fool proof. Now narrow your visual field once more so you can only see the movie screen in your mind and run your film once more. At the point when the film stops allow as many different endings as you can to arise in your thoughts or make them up if you need to. Choose one that seems good to you and give your movie a happy ending. With a little imagination it should be possible for you to modify the above technique to fit many different situations in your life in which you would like to create some modification to your behaviour.

The kind of change we have been discussing so far has been in relation to change within the three bodies and selves that make up a human being. However, there is a kind of outer global change that can occur in your life which it would be fruitful for us to explore in more detail. The kind of global change we are talking about occurs when a person's whole way of living, their fundamental attitude, approach or orientation to life, undergoes a transformation.

Basically there are three different approaches, paths or ways of living that you can adopt during your time on earth. The first is to live life for yourself. A life dominated by the sense of 'I.' The second is to live your life for others. A life dominated by the sense of 'I am not.' The third way is to live neither by the sense of 'I' nor 'I am not' but by surrender to your Soul or God. The third way can only be lived after you have experienced and mastered the first two ways of living. In the western world in general the first way is often presented as the way people should live. Indeed the economic structures of most capitalist societies are based on it. Curiously, considering how abhorrent such a way of living is to most 'enlightened' people, in a great majority of new age and spiritual teachings there is still an enormous emphasis on the first way. You create your own reality and because you do so you can manifest what ever you want in your life. You can be happy, wealthy, healthy, attractive and have any thing you want. All this dominated by the concept of 'I' and what 'I want.' What you want is always based on your sense of self, your ego, the root of your ordinary 'I'ness. There is in the best of such teachings at least some consideration of the effect any such changes will have on the other people in your life. Some also consider the effect of you having what you want on society in general. Realistically it is all very well to want something but could you cope with the changes having it would create. It is a grave error to think that changes in your own personal world only effect you and your immediate circle. The effects can be like the ripples that happen after a stone has been dropped in a pond. They go on and on, spreading wider and wider.

Most of these theories draw analogies from Nature concerning the fact that life itself is abundant. Trees and flowers produce thousands and millions of seeds. The earth is seen to be a planet of plenty. In essence a veritable garden of Eden. The error in this reasoning is that it does not go far enough. It is true that life on Earth is abundant but not in all places equally nor in the same places all the time. Nature has its seasons, its times of growth and times of death. Trees and flowers do produce thousands and millions of seeds, but not all survive and grow to full stature. All flowers, trees and animals cannot flourish everywhere. Some need a lot of sunlight, some a lot of water, others cannot cope with rapid temperature changes and so on. There is a time and place for everything in nature's economy. It is bountiful but it is also specific. You will not find nature trying to grow fir trees in a desert. Your ability to manifest what you want in life is governed by similar considerations.

None of the previous statements is an objection to the idea that you create the world that you live in, your own unique reality or that you can manifest what you want in life. Both are true within certain confines. It is a valuable exercise, before embarking upon a major program of manifestation, to explore the depths of your ego, to discover the true function of the various things that you would wish to manifest in your life. For example, people often say that they want more money but look beneath the surface of that want. What would having more money do for you? Would it help you to stop worrying? Would you feel physically better if you had more money? Do you think it would make you more attractive? Would you get more respect from other people? Will it help you to manifest your dream? Do you simply want more money so that you can buy more material possessions? What would having more possessions mean? Perhaps you might worry more but just about different issues. The way of the self is focused on your inner life, the world within. Living the path of the self both honours and satisfies the needs of your belly. It is the path of youth from about the ages of say twelve to twenty five. This path, could also be called the path of the physical body as it is the needs of the body-self that are the initial basis of all the desires that you seek to fulfil. Later the mind-self and its desires come into play as it tries to interpret the needs of the body-self and frequently gets it wrong. It is extremely important to get to know your mind-self, your ego intimately. The real issue is to make your ego congruent in its desires with the desires and needs of the body self and soul. To know and understand each fully.

Many new age philosophies and eastern spiritual teachings talk of eliminating the ego as something that is inherently bad. This is a dangerous belief and is an avoidance of a problem, not a solution. The solution is to make your ego so strong and complete that it is content to allow you periods of time when it does not govern your actions. Time when your soul can express itself through your everyday life. You could imagine a complete and healthy ego to be like a great cat who, replete after a large meal, just curls up and goes to sleep secure in its knowledge that it can deal with whatever situations might arise and whilst the cat sleeps other animals come out to play. It is vital to explore your own personal power by working to manifest what you want in life so that you can discover the full extent of your power. It is only when you have reached a deep understanding of the basis of your desires by coming to know the needs of both your physical self and your ego self and have brought the two into harmony, and have mastered the skill of manifestation that you can possibly live otherwise.

The second way of living is also one that is extolled by many as 'the' way to live and that way is to deny the self and to live only for others. It is a way of living adopted by as many people as the first way, the way of the self, and often as unsuccessfully. To live for others is to direct your attention away from your self and your needs. It is a way of life that is out in the world. It requires a particular sensitivity to the needs of others if it is to be successful. A deep feeling of empathy and connection is needed with all life outside of the self. Its basis is care and compassion for others. To be a caring person is to consider others. To be compassionate in your dealings with them. The second way could also be called the way of the carer but unfortunately it is nearly always based on a weak ego structure. A feeling of inner emptiness that is filled by making others more important than yourself. The path of the 'other' is related to the period of life between the early twenties and the late forties. It is really the path of the soul and mind combined. A mature mind that is powerfully and finely attuned to the world around it through its contact with the mental consciousness of others as well as its own soul. A mind and ego that having lived for the fulfilment of the needs of the body-self wants to give something back to the world. Unfortunately, in following this path in life it is all too easy to lose your sense of self totally and to be completely unable to motivate yourself into any form of action unless it is of benefit to others. This is a problem of deep importance. If there should come a time in a life lived this way when all the others upon whom it is based are absent perhaps through growing maturity or death, the person is left unable to deal with life having no focus upon which to base it. Yet in spite of the inherent difficulties in this way of living it is vital that you all explore it. It is the way to find your connection to the rest of humanity and indeed the whole of creation. It is this path that satisfies the needs of the heart.

Ultimately neither living for the self nor living for others or even trying to combine both is totally satisfying. Integrating self and other is an important concept but one that cannot be realised because each way will at some point involve a total denial of the other. Each position is fundamentally the polar opposite of the other. Conflict must and will occur. It is certain that at some point the needs of your self will come into profound conflict with the needs of the others in your life. When your love for your self conflicts with your love for others, this is an extremely painful space to be in because neither way can win. Which ever path dominates, only does so at the expense of the other and, as in reality we are talking of two different ways for one person to live, you are always winning and losing simultaneously.

The ideal situation is to live your life for your self when young, then having mastered that path and as you get older and take on the responsibility of a family move on to the path of the other and its mastery and then finally move on from that path to the path of surrender. Having mastered the paths of the 'self' and 'other' and knowing that it is not possible to integrate living for yourself and living for others in any satisfactory fashion, you must surrender both positions and live for the glory of God, the All That Is. This is achieved by allowing your soul and immortal spirit body to express themselves fully in the world. It is only in this way that you can avoid the pain of the inner conflict between the needs of your body-self, the desires of your mind self and your compassion for others. There is absolutely no possibility of doing this unless you have at least for some period of time lived just for yourself, so as to have had the chance to satisfy the needs of your body self and complete your ego. Neither can it be done without having lived for others wherein you satisfied the dictates of your heart and have come to a position in which you know that you are totally interconnected with and interdependent upon everyone else in your life. It is only your soul initially and later your immortal spirit self in their transcendent position beyond physical space and time which have the ability to judge exactly how the events and decisions in your life should unfold so that the needs of everyone in your world can best be met. Nor is this to say that some will not experience loss and pain, even you yourself, but that all things will balance out in the end and all will be satisfied, most likely in ways totally unforeseen and unthought of by you or others.

The path of surrender can only be lived if you **know** that you have a higher self, a soul-self and that you can become an immortal spirit. Belief is not enough. Knowledge that has come through profound personal experience, obtained through some form of spiritually transformative occurrence such as a deep exploration of the awareness work detailed in this book, is what is required. When you know that the soul is real, then and only then, can you surrender. Out of that knowledge and the integration of your whole being your immortal spirit is born. The path of surrender can only be lived fully when your spirit self is fully active. For your mind to surrender to spirit and your higher self and beyond that God, is the act of faith. Faith that everything and everyone will be taken care of. Faith that you live in a merciful reality. There is an old saying concerning

Faith, Hope and Love. Each of these three virtues relates to one of the three ways of living. Love is the essence of the path of the other. Hope is the essence of the path of the self. Faith is the path of surrender.

It is easy to tell when the time has come for you to change from the path that you are currently following, be it the path of the self or the path of the other. You change when it no longer works. If you are following the path of the self, when you find the results of your efforts are something less than rewarding, when the sense of satisfaction in your life is diminishing then you are at a crossroads. You either change to a different path or stubbornly put more and more energy into a way of life that is redundant. If, in your exploration of the path of the self, you are working with manifestation and visualisation techniques it is often the time when the techniques no longer bear fruit. Nor will you be able to find meaningful reasons as to why that should be so. The reality is simple. The techniques are fine it is just that they no longer work for you. You could at this point be called a master of the way of the self. Mastery of any skill always leaves a vast amount of mental energy with no outlet because the challenge is gone from that particular arena. Your choice is to explore another path or struggle with endless frustration if you refuse.

If you follow the path of the other then you know that it has come to an end when you can no longer do it with a good heart. When it no longer brings you the deep contentment that it used to. When whispers of dissatisfaction intrude upon your consciousness such as "Can't they do this for themselves," or "What about me." When these whispers become open anger then you know that this path is ended for you. You can also tell that it is time to change when you no longer seem to be able to 'get it right.' When you do not seem to have that same deep connection that allows you to know exactly what the other person wants at any particular time. In either case, whether you follow the path of the self or the other, when your ability to follow it has ended your only choice is to pursue the opposite path. If you have followed *self* then you must pursue *other*. If you have followed *other* then you must pursue *self*. Remember that you must be a master of both these paths before you can follow the path of surrender. Unfortunately, there is a tendency to try and follow the path of surrender as soon as the first major path that you followed in life comes to an end. A desire born out of fear not out of mastery. To follow either path to its end takes years of work and practise. It is all to easy to think that you are too tired to start over. It seems much simpler to let go and surrender rather than to master the opposite path. Such a choice is not open to you. The path of surrender can only be lived by a personality that has fully explored the other two paths. It is only such a person that can survive the rigours of fulfiling God's will. You must fight the urge to collapse that comes when one path is ended, for following the other path until you have mastered it also is the only course of action open to you. To follow no path at all is to fall into despair, despondency and disillusionment.

Change in the state of your being or in the path you are following in life will always create a change in the quality and content of the consciousness that you generate. Change is essential to life. Please don't fight it. Many people are currently exploring all manner of ways for gaining power and influence and creating change in their lives. You only have to look at the adverts in any periodical to see the endless adverts for the latest in Shamanism, Hypnosis, Positive Thinking, Crystal Empowerment, Life Coaching, Psychic Awareness, Paganism, and many channelled teachings. What next? Surely all their different approaches can not all be right? The truth is all these teachings have at least some valuable insights to offer and as there are at least six billion different mental worlds on the planet Earth alone there is a good chance they are all right, at least for a certain percentage of the earth's population, some of the time!

Behind all these different approaches is the need within the people who attend the courses or who read books like this one to experience some degree of control over their lives, to find some meaning in the suffering they all undergo at different times, but most of all to change themselves and their lives. Most people after some self reflection see their attitudes as the major source of their problems. You could say that at the point when you realise that the real source of most of your problems in life is you yourself you begin to try and change your mind. The problem is that by the time you realise this, your attitudes and beliefs have become so rigid that change has almost become an impossibility for you to achieve by your own efforts. You then have to seek help outside of yourselves through psychotherapists, psychics, healers, spiritual masters, channels and the like. The trouble with this is that whilst the techniques employed by these people do create change, there is an enormously powerful and seductive pull to forget that the truth is the only person who can really change you is you! There can be a tendency for you to come to accept that the power to change comes from without. In fact it is often easier to accept that the power is outside yourself rather than within. There is always someone else to blame then when things do not seem to be working out for you. Perhaps you are no longer in tune with the teachings, or you have evolved and need more advanced teachers or techniques, the list of excuses is endless.

The power of your soul consciousness can, through the force of its impact, create change through the whole of your being. It is like a row of dominoes, knock one over and all the others fall in turn. A flood of soul consciousness that passes through into the physical realm has enormous impact on the physical body. Once integrated into the physical body, any awareness of the physical body will be changed and as the physical consciousness generated impacts the mental body that too is changed, creating further change in the mental consciousness generated, which flows back to the soul through the physical body creating more and more change. Such a scenario is like the long drawn out reverberation of a bell. A situation in which change occurs spontaneously through the impact of the consciousness generated by your finely honed awareness of your own being. This spontaneous change is the true nature of a spiritual revelation in which it is as if the bell of your being was struck at the level of your soul with one mighty blow. The shock waves create change at a fundamental level. Remember, the truth is simple, the power is yours, it is called Love. It is the nature of your soul consciousness and it can and will manifest change through your whole being and life.

The major outer structure in peoples lives that need to change is very often their intimate personal relationships. So let's shine the light of consciousness on this aspect of life next and discover how much new creative awareness we can generate within you in relation to this area of your life.

CHAPTER 6

RELATIONSHIPS

The reality of most relationships is that they are not relationships at all. Most of the behaviour that we call relating is not part of a true relationship. Relating is a connection and communication between two people. It implies an exchange, a moving back and forth. In most relationships all that is happening is that the partners are being internally stimulated in different parts of their being through the proximity of another. Ultimately, through contact with the people in your life you gain a deeper more profound experience of some, or all, of your three selves. Whilst this effect is useful and indeed important as part of the benefit of involvement with other people, it does not constitute a relationship.

Do you remember the first time you fell in love? We are sure that you floated around thinking how wonderful life was and how good you felt. We are also sure that everything inside and outside you seemed bigger and brighter. We can guarantee that at various points you actually said in your mind if not out loud "I am in Love" - not "I am in love with so and so." You were in the presence of your own soul and allowing its light to radiate through you. You did not even see the other person because you were blinded by the brilliance of your own soul consciousness! The truth is that in the beginning you were actually in love with your own soul not the other person. When you first met each other there was an enormous increase in your perception of your feelings, the flow of life energy in your soul body, because of the powerful activation of your soul awareness that occurred. This activation made it impossible for you not to be aware of your own feelings, your life energy. Impossible for you not to be in your soul-self, your higher self. This stimulation at the level of your life energy broke through any barriers to the *love*, the consciousness of your own soul shining through the gateways into the other dimensions of your being.

When you meet certain people you will often find yourself considering spending more time with them because of the way they stimulate you. You may want to have a relationship with them. You may even decide that you love them. However, if you could just remember that most of what is happening is that they trigger an intense degree of self awareness within you, you might manage to avoid all the problems that can arise with saying, "I love you," to them, with all its potential for confusion and pain. If you could just say to the other person when you are in this state, "you seem to be able to bring me into a deep awareness of my own soul," or some such similar statement, it would help enormously. If you can do this your contact with them would be much more real. Your vision would be clear enough to see whether you had the possibility of actually relating harmoniously to the other person at all the different levels of being. Just because someone can give you an experience of your own soul, your own inner love, or indeed any other part of your being, it does not necessarily follow that you could live happily together.

It is quite easy for you to examine the effect of the contact you have with any or all of the people involved in your life by simply asking yourself which parts of your being you feel are stimulated by contact with them. As an example, suppose you want to examine the effect of your contact with your best friend. Ask yourself the following questions or slight variations thereof. Do they stimulate me mentally or emotionally? Do I enjoy doing things with them and being in their physical presence? Do they help me to be in touch with my feelings? Each of the three questions relate to one of the dimensions of your being. In this case your mind, body and soul respectively. You should be able to instantly see which parts of your being are stimulated by the contact between you and your best friend. If they were to do the same exercise the answers could well be quite different to yours. It is vitally important in your quest for spiritual development that all the dimensions of your being are fully activated all the time. For without this you would never be able to develop and integrate your three selves. Bearing this in mind, please do not be tempted to interpret the foregoing as a criticism of the stimulating effect that involvement with other people has in your lives.

When looking at this phenomena of the internal stimulation that occurs through contact with other people it is easy to see how discord can arise. You become attached to people because of the stimulation you receive in their presence. In fact, some of you will ensure that they stay a part of your lives by marrying them. The difficulties arise when for some reason they no longer stimulate your being as they once did, perhaps because you or they have undergone some radical change or growth. When and if that happens you may well end up leaving them and looking elsewhere for that stimulation. Alternatively, you may not look elsewhere but spend many hours talking with your partner about why they no longer stimulate you. Often you end up blaming them for their inadequacy. In this case you may stay with your partner and accept the loss of contact with the part of your being that they stimulated. Though it is unlikely that you will ever be able to let go of that sense of loss completely and that you will, at some level, blame them for it. Then again you may stay with them and seek the necessary activation elsewhere. If you are married this is often a recipe for disaster.

Fundamentally this kind of situation arises because you allow yourself to depend on the people involved in your life to always stimulate certain parts of you. What you should be doing is learning to activate those aspects of your being yourself. Then you do not need to involve yourself with other people just because of the way they stimulate you. When you have reached this stage there is finally a possibility for you to begin truly relating to the people around you. This activation of your being is a vital and natural part of your growth towards total self awareness and the creation of a character. It is simply that most of you will get stuck at this first stage.

To relate to someone is to engage in the exchange and transformation of consciousness. If you bear in mind that consciousness is the carrier of information from the different levels of your being, then to relate to another is to communicate with another—the truest, purest form of communication possible. A true relationship is always a two way process. You give of your own consciousness and partake of that of another. We have already stated that a human being exists in three different dimensions simultaneously and can generate the particular qualities of consciousness appropriate to each dimension depending upon which 'self' or 'body' awareness is functioning within. We will, throughout the rest of this chapter, use the terms, 'relationship' and 'relating' interchangeably. In reality, we are only concerned with the act of relating. Indeed, if you talk too much in your everyday life about your 'relationships' then you can be certain that your relating to others is not going well. If it was, you would not be talking about it, you would be living it! To talk endlessly of a relationship is to discuss that which is no longer active. It is as if you are standing aside, separate, and dissociated. It is rather like discussing the dissection of a corpse, or being a vulture picking over the bones of a dead animal. It is important to remember that a relationship is not an entity or a thing that you can possess. You cannot *have* a relationship with someone else, you can only relate to them. A relationship is not an object to possess it is a dynamic process of communication.

The most instructive thing you can do when looking at all human relating is to look at it from the point of view of consciousness and communication. In doing so you can instantly see they either work or they do not. You are either in relationship with someone or you are not. There is nothing in-between these two states—the state of relating or that of not relating. To use an energetic terminology we could say the energy is either flowing or it is not. A relationship as some kind of separate entity with a life of its own cannot actually exist, being a description of a static energy state, an isolated phenomenon. The universe does not support isolated phenomena. If consciousness is not flowing in a relationship then it is no longer a relationship because the exchange and transformation of information is damaged and any further possibilities for the growth and spiritual development of the people involved is ended. The fundamental reason for relating to other people in life is so that you can grow into your own understanding and experience of your self and your connection with God. It also gives you endless opportunities to transform your consciousness. You achieve this by making the relating that you do with others as joyful as possible.

Relating operates with connections, interaction and communication at all levels of consciousness and being. You can look at any of your relating to others and see, without too much difficulty, what levels are operating. The more levels that are connected, the greater the possibilities for growth and transformation. However, it is common for you to be relating at more levels than you are consciously aware. Few people are aware of the soul level connections that are part of their daily lives. Do not get too carried away when analysing all your interactions. You could end up deluding yourself into thinking that you have less contact and communication with the people in your life than is actually the case!

It is possible to explore all your current relationships with others by looking at which qualities of consciousness are interconnected. Any relationship will have communication, at the very least, at one level of being. Be it the soul, physical or mental. It may have communication occurring at two levels or even three simultaneously. For example, let us say that Joe is relating to Mary. They have enjoyable, and occasionally profound, sexual experiences together. They enjoy a number of similar sporting activities, eating out and they are both fond of animals. They also experience periods of comfortable silence when they each feel a profound sense of wellness in each others presence, as well as periods of intense feeling when they are both easily moved to tears by, for example, a beautiful sunset. From this brief exploration of their relating to each other which levels of being and consciousness would you say are connected? The answer in their case is that they are communicating at the physical and soul levels of being. Their involvement in the physical sensations of touching, eating, drinking and movement are indicative of the interaction of physical consciousness, of communication between their body selves. The connection at the soul level of being is indicated by the harmony of feeling that they experience with each other. Remember that by feeling we mean the reaction and interaction of the life energy in the soul body, not emotion. In this particular example there is little interaction at their mental levels of beingness. However, in this case it is not a problem or issue for them as long as they are content with the situation as it is. Though in the future, should one feel the need to share in the consciousness created by their mental body, and discover that this is not possible then a problem of basic incompatibility at the mental level of being may arise.

When you look more deeply at your relating to others it can be tempting to say that consciousness is not connected and flowing in a situation which is characterised by arguments and distrust. However, this is not the case. These things often indicate a level of relating in which the connection is very intense. It is a mistake to assume that a powerful flow of consciousness between two people has to manifest as peace and harmony. The actual way in which the relating manifests is often governed by the mental selves or egos of the two people involved. However, in a relationship between people who have achieved a degree of integration between the different dimensions of their being, you can be sure that the kind of interaction that is occurring between them will reflect the understanding of the higher selves of the people involved. An understanding of the kind of experience needed and the lessons that have to be learnt in order that their lives can fulfil their unique position in the universe. When consciousness is not connected and flowing, when there is no relating or stimulation, the most common practical manifestation will be a quality of indifference between the people concerned. If the people in this scenario are still actually living together then it will most likely be for other reasons outside the actual relationship between the two people involved e.g. because of children, financial reasons, cultural mores and so on. Whilst many people in these sort of circumstances might feel that they could still continue growing towards spiritual unity the truth is they are stuck. Growth can only happen when consciousness is flowing and when Love is an active force within your being, when you are relating fully to the people around you.

There are many problems and confusions that can arise in your relating to others. Problems that are specific to different levels or dimensions of your being. If we look first at the problems that are unique to the soul dimension then probably the major problem is around Love. Surprisingly, considering the primary role that most of you probably feel that it has in your relating to others, we would suggest that 'love' in itself has no deep meaning or significance in your relating. The fact is that for most of you love is little more than a mental concept or set of opinions that you hold concerning the emotions that you expect to feel when you are relating to someone. Most of these emotions are usually associated more with the experience of the activation of your self as we outlined it earlier than with the act of relating. The reality is that Love is in your soul. It is simply what and who you are in that dimension. You have much of your being in Love. To be in love, you must be Love. The nature of your soul consciousness is Love. You are Love when your soul consciousness shines through you, affecting all the dimensions of your being and outward towards others from your soul body. Only when you are Love, are you a truly radiant being. Love has very little to do with relationships. In your relating to other people your love is meaningless, it simply is. Your love has no real relevance to anyone except you. It will not necessarily change anyone else. The power of Love is power for the self, your self. It can only change you. Your Love, your soul self and it's consciousness has impact on the people you relate to, but it is only their own love that will truly change them.

For most of you we expect that Love has great meaning but that meaning is probably based around a mental concept of Love as an active verb 'to love' instead of its proper usage which is 'to be Love.' No doubt in your current relationships to love another and to be loved by another means many things; that you will live together, that you will get married, that you will be faithful to each other, that you will take care of each other, that you will love no other. We are sure you could add many more to your own list of the different things that 'to love' another person means. Yet all of this is a total misunderstanding of the true nature of Love and its place in your relationships. Good relating is based on the connection of consciousness and its manifestation in such practical things as understanding, empathy, consideration, honesty, compassion and clear communication. It is infinitely more important that you like and are open with the people that you choose to relate to rather than that you love them. Please remember that Love is simply what you are. Don't clutter it with too many thoughts. The connection you have with the other people in your life should not be based on Love except that ideally it occurs between people who are manifesting as radiant beings of Love.

Like love, 'caring' is another area that confuses many people. There is in everyone a great need to 'care for' another human being. It is very important that you do not confuse this with 'care about' another human being. To care about another human being is a natural part of relating well to them. It is dependent on the level of contact and communication that you have with the other person. However, the need to care for

118

another is the undisguised operation of the soul's seeking for 'oneness.' The need to 'care for' another person is often decried in many psychological models as a neurotic substitute for the inability to care for yourself. Yet from the soul's perspective of oneness if you are one with another then to care for them is to care for yourself for there is no separation between you. However, pragmatically speaking, the fact that within yourselves you are often separate from your own body and soul means that 'caring for' another can become a way of not dealing with your inability to care for yourself.

Many people feel called to heal others, which is simply another way of caring for them and again this can be a neurotic way of avoiding healing and caring for your self. However, if you can allow your caring for, or healing of another, no matter how distorted or neurotic your egoic need to do so may be, to reach down into the deepest levels of your being, into your soul, then it will transform you. In essence, you do this by maintaining a strong perception of the true soul basis of the act of caring for another. Your caring for others will then become part of your spiritual practice and will help you to expand your link with your higher self, keep the gateways open and the path clear. These needs or desires and many other ones of a similar nature are whispers from your soul as it seeks to become one with all the dimensions of your own being and that of others.

The major problem in the physical realm that creates difficulties in relating is human sexuality. Sexual difficulties, which perhaps many of you feel are the major problem area in your relating, are dealt with in the next chapter. The mental realm is in many ways the source of most, if not all, problems that occur within relationships because many of you will, in all probability, be living your life predominately from the mental dimension of your being. The mind also dominates in relating to another because of its pre-eminent role in the basic act of communication which is usually perceived as being synonymous with verbal communication or speech. In what follows we will explore a number of different problems that stem from the mental realm and the ego-self. However, we would not expect you to have problems in all of the areas, nor will we discuss them in any particular order.

Personal power is a major problem in some relationships. To be able to explore this issue properly we must first define what we mean by 'power.' The clearest and simplest definition of power in your relating to others is that it is concerned with decision making. The decisions can range from what kind of clothing to buy, to the particular food the couple eat, to where they live and the way they earn a living. These are decisions concerning external issues. There are, of course, decisions relating to internal issues such as the way they relate to each other, the beliefs and opinions that they hold and so on. A great deal of time and energy is wasted in relationships where each person is trying to exert their power of decision over the other. Such struggles are nearly always based on the 'I am right' or 'I know best' syndromes. One of the partners decides that they know more about, or understands more clearly, a particular issue and sets out to enforce their perception on their partner. Now of course it is quite possible that they do understand the situation better than their partner but we can guarantee that by the time they have finished trying to validate their position their partner feels dumb, ignorant and totally inadequate. The partner who gets their own way in the decision making process is often left with a hollow, empty feeling inside, "but I did not mean to upset you, you know I love you, I only wanted what I felt was best." Few people enjoy the power struggles in their relationships. Both parties nearly always end up feeling bad. Life is about making decisions but it is also about having fun.

Ultimately, what most people intend to manifest as 'power for' their partner ends up coming out as 'power over' them. At various times in your life you need the security of someone having power for you, making decisions on your behalf because you are unable to do it for yourself due to fear or disability of some kind. To have power for another human being is a great responsibility as well as being an amazing gift. To exert power on some one else's behalf is to give yourself the opportunity to explore the 'Warrior's Heart,' to raise the sword of freedom on their behalf. The way of the warrior is a fascinating phenomenon. The chance to explore it has to a great extent seemingly disappeared from the modern world. Yet, it is still possible to do so in your everyday relationships. The warrior is essentially someone who uses their personal power to thwart the forces that stand against the person they are defending. They stand for some or all of the great values of Truth, Justice, Beauty and Freedom.

Independence is another crucial issue in relationships. Independence is perhaps the major life issue that people actually avoid exploring by relating to others. Yet, it is the one area on which all relationships can founder upon sooner or later. To be independent is to be totally self reliant. To know that the only person who can provide you with the things that you need in life is you. You are the only person who can give you totally unconditional love. You are the only person you can trust completely. You are the only person who can be totally consistent in terms of feelings and emotions. You are the only person who can truly reassure you. You are the only person who will always need you no matter what! We are sure that at this point there is a part or all of you saying that this is all rubbish, but it isn't. It is all true. In simple terms being independent is knowing that the only person who can make you happy or sad is you! The responsibility is yours.

Now we know that this probably sounds like a very heavy emotional burden to your ego, but this particular self-realisation is perhaps the most liberating of all. If it is all down to you, then you can change anything in your life because you don't have to try and change, or convince of the need to change, anyone who happens to be a part of it, except yourself of course! You can expend all of that emotional energy you would have used on the other person on yourself. You won't even have to deal with resistance. After all why shouldn't you change. It is not a problem for you, is it? You don't think you are going to lose something by changing, do you? You know that it is all down to you, don't you? You really are an independent self actualised person, aren't you? Well perhaps you are not self actualised yet but if you begin to explore these questions you will find yourself well and truly on the path to the full integration of your three selves.

Being independent is not blaming someone else for something that is your responsibility. The truth is, and you already know this, it is all your responsibility. You created it all. Only you can change it all. Most relationships are so constructed as to prevent any kind of realisation concerning the nature of independence. This is because they are based on one person providing for certain of the other person's needs and vice versa. These relationships are a bargain wherein neither person must grow out of their dependency on the other if it is to last. Should one of the parties actually grow out of the need for the other to provide for them, the bargain can no longer be upheld, both partners will begin to feel dissatisfied, and ultimately the relationship will fail. If the partner who has achieved a measure of independence stays with the relationship they will most probably feel resentful that their partner still expects them to provide their side of the bargain even though they will be getting nothing in return any more. Inevitably, they will tire of providing for their partners needs and refuse to do so. They will then be accused of not loving their partner because they no longer provide the required emotional support and so on. At this stage the end of the relationship is very definitely in sight. Sometimes, the partner in the above scenario who is still dependent, will often seek elsewhere for their needs to be met as soon as they sense any change in the bargain, to find someone who in their terms 'really' loves them. In reality someone who will provide them with the same emotional support that they still need but have lost in their existing relationship.

Another issue in relating to others, and it is intertwined with power and independence, is 'identity.' Most people conceive of their identity as 'what' rather than 'who' they perceive themselves to be. An identity is nearly always seen to be a composite structure. You probably identify with your sex, your job, your children and so on. Yet the nature of your identity is very simple, you are a human being. Most peoples identity is not rooted in their fundamental human nature but is composed almost entirely in their perception of their ability to perform certain roles in life. In reality any identity that does not fully encompass your fundamental identity is false. It is but a mask. Your identity is the answer to the question "Who are you?" Ask yourself this question now. What was your reply? If you are truly who you are then your answer will have been "I am me." In fact the question will somehow feel oddly meaningless. Once you know who you are it is of no more interest to you. It is done. You are you, and that is it!

For many, the question of who you are, your identity, is a constant seeking to get others to recognise what, rather than who, you are. Erroneously believing that 'what' you are is your identity. Much of your relating to other people will be taken up with playing certain roles and trying to get the other people to identity them. A sophisticated every day version of the game of charades. Sometimes in charades the players fail to recognise the identity being acted out, in which case the person acting out the particular role wins. In this real life version of the game, the situation is just the opposite. The person acting out the role must have it identified by the other people otherwise they, the actor, lose. For example, in relating to your best friend, who is experiencing some problem in their life, you begin to act out one of your identities which we will say is the part of a sympathetic friend. In fact, it may be your primary identity in life generally. However, they do not respond to your act. They refuse to discuss their problem thereby not acknowledging your primary identity. If this happens your identity is shattered and at this point in your relating to your friend you become angry, hurt and extremely confused because you are no longer certain who you are. Your whole world feels like it is crumbling around you and unless you get the acknowledgement, the recognition you need, your ability to relate to your best friend is seriously jeopardised and may well end. This kind of scenario is played out endlessly in all human relationships in which the people involved confuse their true identify with what they do or more accurately the roles that they play. The reality is even worse than the above example when you realise that, for the most part, in any relationship more than one person is playing a real life charade at the same time, with every one desperate to be identified and validated.

It might be instructive for you to write a list of all the different roles that you play in your relating to others. Once you have made a complete list you can then decide which roles are being validated and which ones are not. Can you identify a primary role? Usually, if a role that you are playing is not being validated in a particular relationship in your life, then you will in all probability experience it as a difficult or problematic relationship. Indeed, you may well find that you decide to finish relating to that particular person. On the other hand you may try to get that particular role validated elsewhere. Sometimes, this will actually improve the original relationship. When a role you are playing in relating to another person is not validated by them it creates enormous pressure and tension in both parties. So, if you get that validation elsewhere the pressure is released and the relationship may improve. You may even find that if they were withholding the recognition of your role, as part of a power play that when you drop the issue, because it is being satisfied elsewhere, that they also finally begin to support your role. However, if they were withholding because they simply could not see you in that particular light then that will not change but at least it will not be such a serious problem any more.

As long as you realise that your true identity has nothing to do with the roles that you play you could perhaps begin to play them purely for fun. Try seeing yourself literally as an actor in the play that is your life. An actor who plays many parts in the same play but who does it for the sheer pleasure and enjoyment of the acting. In life your performance should be done for fun as opposed to an actor in a stage play who does it for the adulation and the money. It is also important to remember that even the very best stage plays have some good and some bad reviews. You won't feel hurt if you do not take it too seriously. Who you really are is how you feel when you are not on the stage of life. Your true identity will become clearer and more concrete to you if you work with all the understanding and exercises offered in this book. Basically just remember that Love is what you are and awareness is the surest route to discovering who you are.

Have you experienced any of the following; anxiety around loss of security, losing a partner, loss of control, loss of independence, falling in love, speaking out, being yourself, being responsible, being loveable, being vulnerable, anxiety around sexuality, bodily functions, your intelligence, your appearance or physique and so on. In short, is your relating dominated by Fear. Fears are always around something that might be going to happen. In reality the only thing that is actually happening in the present is the emotion of fear itself and the mental projection of the future on which it is based. Change the projection from a negative to a positive and watch the fear disappear. In fact better still, eliminate any projection and concentrate on exactly what you are doing. If you maintain a negative projection of the future, about which you are anxious and fearful, then you can be sure that you will be looking diligently for things in your relating to others that will support your projections. Before you know where you are the projection will be reality and the fear won't just be in your mind. The event you are afraid of will actually come to pass. Fear is a disembodied emotion that is based upon lack of physical action. Fear only occurs when there is dissociation from the body. If you are afraid, simply do something, anything, and you will find that the fear dissolves. There is no bodily response to an external circumstance that can be labelled as fear. The sensation you label as fear is a blocking of response, a blocking of physical activity, a refusal to allow movement to flow. Fear is a phenomena of civilisation. It does not exist in the same way in primitive societies where you either fight or you run like hell! If you run and escape you feel elated, exhilarated. I made it! If you fight and conquer then you experience exhilaration and elation also. The other possibility is that you lose the fight and die. In either situation fear does not occur. It is only modern man who blocks his response to situations because he is so civilised. Fear is the great inhibitor. It will prevent you from experiencing all the joy that life offers. It will prevent you from fulfiling relationships. It will keep you from finding the experience of your soul. Many times you will have been advised to confront your fears but it is not your fears that have to be confronted, it is your refusal to act. In life you have two choices, you either fight or run. You live or you just barely exist.

Any exploration of relationships would not be complete without looking at specific soul relationships. The love you experience as you connect with your higher self is the only totally unconditional love that you will ever experience or ever need to. To experience this kind of inner love fully is to become a radiant being. It is a place from which you can relate for the sheer joy of relating. The definition of a soul relationship is one that involves two people who have good contact with their higher selves, who constantly have within them the experience of that pure unconditional love, who are illuminated by that love or soul consciousness and who exchange it freely between themselves so that when they come together they simply bask in each others radiance. In this kind of relationship the two people could truly be said to enlighten and enliven each other.

The Twinsoul and Soulmate relationships, the specific dynamics of which we will describe in detail shortly, are uniquely powerful 'soul' relationships' but even they are not based on Love, except that as we said, they only work fully when each person is a being in Love. As relationships they are based on the resonant harmonics of oneness—the oneness of the fundamental nature of the soul, the life energy. In a soul relationship it can be said that you are not in love with each other but that you are most certainly one with each other simply because you are each manifesting Love, the light of your soul consciousness throughout all the dimensions of your being. Soul relationships are based on the dynamics of oneness not on love. Love is an individual concern. It is your soul consciousness. Oneness is a universal soul quality. There is only one life energy and its need is to resonate, vibrate, pulsate, and express joy.

One of the fundamental properties of relating to others is that they offer you the chance to see and experience yourself as you really are. All the people that you relate to in your everyday life are mirrors for you. The only way to learn about yourself is through relating to other people and life. It is very easy to come to the conclusion that you are a wonderful balanced highly evolved human being when you are not relating to anyone. Living on a mountain top in meditation is not the only way to avoid relating to people, many people manage to make their own homes a mountain top. Even their minds can become the mountain upon which they hide from themselves. In all your relationships you are looking into mirrors that have varying degrees of clarity. The more levels of your being that are connected in a relationship the better the mirror. Your deepest need is to see *all* of yourself as you really are.

A twinsoul is someone whose seed pattern within their soul body is a near perfect match for your own. Relating to your twinsoul offers you the chance to experience perfect resonance, to feel an almost total harmony of ideas, beliefs, opinions and goals with another human being. This is because the seed pattern is the fundamental organising factor that ultimately structures all your internal forces and consciousness. A person whose seed pattern is a perfect match for your own will have an incredible degree of similarity in their overall make up. This might sound as if we are saying that they are exactly the same but this is never the case, as each person's individual life experiences will be quite dissimilar. This will create many subtle but significant differences, more than enough to supply you with all the joy and excitement that you normally experience when exploring the possibilities of any new intimate human relationship. Your twinsoul is the most perfect mirror you can ever experience. All your relationships allow you to see different aspects of yourself, but few of you are ready or willing to experience the total depth and clarity offered to you by looking into the mirror of a relationship with your twinsoul. Often it is quite painful enough to see yourself in all the partial mirrors that the other people in your life offer.

Energetically the kind of resonance that occurs between you and your twinsoul intensifies the activity of your life energy enormously with an equivalent increase in the vibrancy and impact of your soul consciousness, your love. The partners in a twinsoul relationship are a trigger for each other's life energy and consciousness. They inspire each other. One partner, when excited, can entrain a similar response in their partner. Then, as they both vibrate together at the same frequency, that excitement bounces back and forth between the two which excites their energies even more. Their joy and excitement spirals higher and higher. This phenomena, which is called resonance in the physical realm, occurs as two vibrating objects, having the same innate frequency, are brought in to close proximity to each other. Through resonance the amplitude of the energetic wave form they emit will increase enormously up to the limit that their structures can withstand. This energetic resonance between twinsouls is illustrated in figure 13. In the physical realm if the resonance continues for too long the amplitude of the energy will be become so great that the vibrating objects can disintegrate. This is how it is possible for an opera singer to shatter a glass. They sing a note that is at the same natural frequency that the glass vibrates at, thereby forcing the glass to vibrate. A resonance is then established between their voice and the vibrating glass. The energy or amplitude of the wavelength of the note then increases as they continue singing until finally the glass shatters when its structure can no longer deal with the stress of the steadily increasing vibration. In most cases it is the glass that shatters rather than the opera singer's vocal chords and body because they, being made of flexible material, are better able to deal with the great energy created! Overall, the structure of a human being is able to cope with enormous excitation which is just as well for all the twinsoul relationships that already exist on the Earth.

In our discussion of the nature of the soul we spoke of how the seed pattern in the soul body has an overall quality of either expansion or contraction, which is definitive of its fundamental nature. With this in mind it should be obvious that if your twinsoul is a soul whose seed pattern is exactly the same as your own, then your soulmate is someone whose seed pattern is in exactly the opposite state of contraction or expansion. Relating to your soul mate gives you the opportunity to experience the full realisation of your potential as a human being. They give you the possibility of manifesting all the qualities of beingness that are latent within your soul. A relationship with your soul mate gives you the opportunity to experience how having a seed pattern in its exact opposite state of manifestation would colour your life and experience. The energetic resonance that occurs between soul mates is shown in figure 14, where the superimposition creates a filling out of the waveform which represents the fundamental nature of each. This is unlike the phenomenon of opposites as it occurs in wave form mechanics in the physical realm where exact opposites actually cancel each other out.

Figure 13

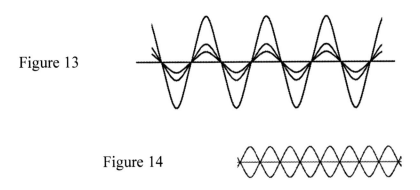

Figure 14

Relating to your soul mate and twin soul are not the only paths to activating your potentials or experiencing who you really are. You can achieve the same ends through meditation, self reflection and relating to many different people who will both activate and show you all the different parts of your soul. It is just that these other ways require a great degree of determination and the ability to integrate many different experiences. Curiously, we can assure you that many of you are in actual fact already in very close contact with your soul mate without you even realising it. The key to this lies in the fact that even though your soul may be having a great time communicating with a soul mate in that plane of existence, that if you have very poor contact with your own soul, you will never experience what is actually happening at that level. Sometimes the gateways are so blocked that the huge increase in activity at the soul level just does not flow through and affect the body or mind. Many of you may also have had contact with your twinsoul but the likelihood is that the relating between you was so powerful and painful that you could not maintain it for long though it is unlikely that you do not at least continue to have some form of contact with them. In reality, it is never difficult to find either a twinsoul or soulmate because one or both are somewhere nearby all the time. This is due to the extraordinary attractive power of the life energy of the soul. The force of oneness.

The great majority of people have the desire for a relationship that operates at as many levels as possible. How often have you heard someone say that they wanted someone in their lives with whom they could share everything, 'Mr or Ms.Right.' How often have you said or thought it yourself? This desire for the perfect partner and a relationship that operates at all levels, is the voice of your soul seeking to awaken you to the possibility of a perfect union within your self. A union between all the levels of your being. A union that would mean you have a perfect connection with your higher self. When you achieve this level of inner relationship on all levels it always manifests outwardly in the form of a perfect relationship with another similarly unified human being. The relating between two people who have achieved a full mental, physical and soul body integration can be a uniquely stable base from which to explore the many and diverse opportunities that life offers for experiencing joy and happiness. It can be one of the best relationships in which to discover what each of you can be. It is also something well worth aiming for in life.

Up until now we have focused on the inner relationships in a human being as well as the outer relationships between people but it is time we looked at a being with which we all have a profound relationship. In many ways it is the fundamental relationship throughout life. It is a relationship that you have from the moment of your birth to the time of your death and sometimes even after that. It is your relationship with the planet that you live on, the Earth. Remember that in the first chapter we said that the Earth itself is a conscious being, though of a form quite different to mankind. It should be obvious that just as you can enter into a relationship with another human being, the essential nature of which is the flow and transformation of consciousness, so too you can enter into a dynamic relationship with the Earth. Indeed, it is an essential part of your own spiritual development and self transformation that you do so. The Earth is in a sense a more highly evolved life form than man. It's consciousness is inherently more stable and its integration much better. It is much more in touch with the rest of the universe than man is. It too exists in many different dimensions and has it's own soul pattern within its body of life energy, its soul, the actual structure of which is essentially the same as man's, a double helix. This means that any time you do a soul body gateway clearance, either as a visualisation, or as the hands on version or even when you just focus deeply on your feelings, the resonance between you and the Earth is strengthened. It means that you will begin to experience a deepening in your understanding of and respect for the Earth. You will begin to have a clearer experience of it as a fully aware being. It is also likely that you will find yourself unable to engage in, or be party to, any form of action that is destructive to the Earth and it's resources. In reality there is no separation between the planet, you and the rest of the universe. Somewhere a child dies, a river dries up, a star is born and you experience it all, as does the planet. The consciousness of man and planet intertwine. The gateways between the various bodies of the Earth are what many of you have recognised as natural power spots. These gateways serve the same purpose as the gateways of your own body that are worked with in the various clearing exercises in this book. Power spots are places where you can most easily tap into planetary consciousness. The fundamentally empowering effects for a human being of spending time in such a place is that it will, through the impact of planetary consciousness upon your three bodies, enhance your internal integration and spiritual development. At these places the communication is clearer, your soul consciousness becomes attuned very precisely to the vibrations of planetary soul consciousness and communication takes place. Consciousness flows and you are moved. The planet is also moved as it responds to you. If you can still your mind, if you can increase your awareness of your whole being and all that is around you, if you can open your hearts it will allow a relationship to develop. You will hear the music of the spheres and be aware of the harmonious interaction of all things. Then any discord that occurs will be felt much more keenly and the power for change will be in your hands. You may also begin to experience the being of the Earth in a very direct and tangible fashion in as much as you will become sensitive to what the Earth itself is feeling and experiencing.

You will probably find yourself periodically drawn to the location of power spots and your increased sensitivity will also tell you when to leave such an area as overexposure can have an adverse affect on you. The adverse effect stems from the fact that every human being has a limit on their ability to handle the great increase in the amount of consciousness impacting upon them at such places. Too much exposure can, so to say, literally blow the circuit breakers in your being because it can cause a disruption in the spatial superimposition of your three bodies actually creating a lack of integration.

At this period in Earth's history many people seem to view the relationship between mankind and the Earth as a healing one. There is a common thread running through many current spiritual teachings to the effect that one of your major tasks as human beings is to heal the planet. The ecological or green movement is a powerful trend in politics and society as a whole. Throughout all these teachings there is a curious lack of appreciation of the reality of the situation which is that it is mankind that has made the Earth ill and still continues to do so. In some teachings there is too great a focus on the actual esoteric ritual aspects of healing the planet. It is not enough to visit power spots and there to acknowledge the Earth Mother through prayer or perform planetary healing rituals. Being an armchair ecologist is not good enough. Practical changes must take place in your life. You must live in harmony with the Earth and discontinue any actions that deplete and pollute its natural resources.

The Earth is not sick through self created problems within its own being. It is sick through mankind's own actions. The reality at this stage is not so much that we must 'heal' the Earth but that we need to prove to the great being that is our home planet that we deserve to be allowed to continue living on it. It is also true that the state of our connection with our soul is just as important as our actions in showing the Earth that we deserve a place on it. It is well to remember that it is not the soul body of human beings or their soul consciousness that is causing problems for the planet. All the planetary pollution is being caused by people who are out of contact with their soul, their higher selves. These people have no integration between the different dimensions of their being. It is, in fact, quite difficult for the planet itself to perceive clearly what is causing it so many problems at this point in time due to the differences between the physical and mental consciousness of planetary beings and human beings. This is lucky for mankind because if it could we would find that the Earth was very intolerant of our presence and our abuse. The Earth's current awareness of us is no greater than our awareness of the micro-organisms that live on the skin of our own physical body.

It is important to realise that the physical body of the Earth like the human body has amazing cleansing and self healing capabilities and that it is able to deal with a phenomenal amount of pollution and still maintain balance. However, if we do not make a serious effort to repair the damage that we have caused, the enormously powerful immune system of the planet will become fully aroused and we will be wiped off the face of the planet by varying forms of natural holocausts ranging from earthquakes, and massive droughts to extreme atmospheric changes. Happily, from the planet's perspective, less drastic measures may also serve its need because the amount of pollution occurring physically in the world and within consciousness itself, is creating an environment in which the ability of human kind to simply survive within it is already in serious doubt. Witness the huge increase in stress related disorders and diseases of over taxed immune systems. Even our own bodies are crying out for

130

change, an ending of some kind. Another possibility is that the planet itself might allow the germination of some new and incredibly potent form of bacteria or virus totally inimical to human life. It could also briefly in terms of its own life span, representing a period of perhaps a few hundred human years, stop all it's own self healing activities, so that the human species destroys itself through its own blindness. In fact, there are already signs that this is the case—witness the hole in the ozone layer. If we were more integrated with our soul nature, and provided that our mental self does not dominate our being, we would not be able to abuse the planet as we do because we would immediately sense the effect of our actions on the planet through the communication that is possible via the channel of soul consciousness.

To be able to heal the damage that we have done to the planet it is vitally important to develop an understanding of the planetary ecology. This does not just mean an understanding of the inter-relationships between all the life forms that live on the Earth but also the relationship of these life forms to the Earth and of the Earth to the rest of the solar system and ultimately it's relationship with the whole universe. It is only with this deep understanding of our place in the scheme of things that it is possible to initiate the most effective action towards maintaining the ecological balance of the planet. This understanding is not an intellectual one. It is obtained through a deep feeling of connection with the soul body, the life energy of the Earth. This understanding can only come when a person is fully in tune with their soul body. Without this connection many well meaning efforts to remedy the pollution of the Earth will only create further difficulties. If actions aimed at helping the planet do not come from an intense sense of connection with the life energy of the planet; if the reasons for trying to control pollution spring from self seeking financial or business considerations rather than a true soul connection then the right means will work in the wrong way and ultimately more harm than good will result. It is only with our ability to interpret the information carried by our own and the planet's soul consciousness that we can see the true results of our actions in the physical realm in advance, because the universe of the soul, where soul consciousness is created, is not bound by time. Oddly enough, as many people work on planetary healing it is more likely that humankind will be wiped off the face of the planet by various natural holocausts through the stimulation of planetary awareness and the planetary immune system response that this work creates. Obviously this is not really the intent of the people who do this work but in many cases their soul link is too weak and their actions are often inappropriate. Ultimately, it is important to balance any direct planetary healing work with the actual physical cleansing of the surface itself so that mankind can still continue living safely on it but always this work must be guided by the true voice of the soul not the mental body's emotional position.

It is well to be aware that human consciousness generated by a mind that is selfish, ignorant and soul bereft is as great a pollutant of the planet as all the chemical wastes of all the manufacturing industries. The physical body of the Earth has a hugely powerful self healing capability. However, the mental body of the planet does not have as great a capacity for self healing. Even though the Earth finds it difficult to decode the information carried by the mental consciousness of a human being it still finds it difficult to cope with the actual impact of this kind of consciousness when it is encoded with negativity, pain and fear. These are the worst pollutants of all because they directly effect the mental body and mind energy of the Earth itself. If changes do not take place very soon, both in the degree of integration within human beings and in their connection with the planet, as well as practical physical change in the way the Earth is treated then the planet itself will have to take drastic action to resolve the situation. This will mean the total destruction of the species that is the problem—man! Sadly, many other species will also die should this happen but no more than mankind has already destroyed. So please remember that the truth is, the planet only needs healing because of our presence on it in the first place. Action in both inner attitudes as well as outer behaviour is needed if the problem is to be resolved.

In its ideal form a soul level relationship with the Earth, indeed with the whole of the universe, is encapsulated in the word 'Guardianship.' The concept of guardianship is that the Earth itself is our guardian just as we are the guardian of the life forms upon the Earth that are less advanced than man—namely the plant and animal kingdoms. Guardianship describes an attitude of being and a whole way of living and relating to the Earth and all its flora and fauna and including the rest of mankind. It also describes the attitude that more evolved beings, of which the Earth is one, adopt towards all less evolved forms of life. To be a guardian is to protect something, to look after it, to keep it safe, to shield it, as well as to give it the space in which to grow and mature albeit within certain boundaries. It also describes the higher self's attitude and behaviour when given the permission it needs to act.

The Earth itself discharges its obligation to mankind and all other lesser beings upon it effortlessly. Something that is certainly not true for most human beings. One way you can explore your own position in creation as a guardian is by creating, tending and becoming a guardian of a small piece of land, a garden. If you allow the consciousness of your higher self to express itself through you and then enter into a direct contact with the Earth you are entering in to a profound relationship with the consciousness of the other life forms, namely the plants that are grown in and the creatures that live in the garden you create. In this relationship, as in one between two people, the return flow of consciousness is present and the transformation is there both for your self and those under your care or guardianship. They grow and you grow. To enter into this kind of relationship with a strong clear perception of the fact that to be a guardian of a piece of the Earth, no matter how small, with a constant awareness of the greatness of the consciousness of Gaia, the collective consciousness of all the mineral, plant and animal kingdoms combined, as represented microcosmically in a garden, is to experience a profound transformation. It is different to sending love to another human soul, but of equal importance, because you are then helping the planet to fulfil it's own function as a guardian.

It is vital for you to connect with the planet so that you can learn how the Earth performs it's function as one of the guardians of mankind and that once you understand the principles of 'guardianship' you can use this knowledge in all your relationships. It is the guardian relationship between mankind and those for whom it is mankind's job to guard that is being so badly corrupted. The Earth itself provides us with the space in which to live and grow but we refuse to see it. It shows how we should act so as to discharge our responsibility to the other beings in our care. We are like difficult children who refuse all love and guidance. We can do much to repair this situation by fulfiling our role as a guardian.

All this is not to say that you should immediately go out and create a garden, which is not easy if you live in a block of flats or in a skyscraper, but that you should create for yourself the opportunity to get out and experience the Earth in all its forms and moods. Visit more power spots. Your own higher self is always more than willing to help you in gaining a deep and profound appreciation of the planetary consciousness of the Earth. You can also experience your role as a guardian through relating to animals. To rear an animal, be it dog, cat or any other domestic animal is to experience your role as guardian in the care of the animal. In terms of experiencing what it is like to be a guardian, as well as learning the actual skills involved, animals can be wonderfully potent teachers. Finally, rearing a child is one of the most powerful relationships in which to practice being a guardian. Though it must be said that it is not a relationship in which one should try and learn how to become one. To use children in that way is grossly unfair on them. It is wise to learn the skills of a guardian before becoming a parent!

The teeming life on Earth is created through one fundamental creative process. That process is sexuality. We have already pointed out that it can be a major problem area in your personal relationships and so, to complete our exploration, we must explore this process in relation to human beings in some detail.

CHAPTER 7

SEXUALITY

In this chapter we we are going to explore what is perhaps the major problem in human relationships, namely sexuality. This is a whole area of difficulty for many people requiring a healing of both attitude and physical function. In spite of the changes in modern Western society and its collective attitude over the last few decades, sex is still one of the biggest problem areas in relationships. It is also seen in a very negative light in many spiritual teachings. The truth is that the sexual forces within you are one of the main ways that your soul consciousness draws people into your life. It is the force that the soul uses when manifesting its physical form. Soul consciousness creates new life in the physical realm through human sexuality. The sexual drive is therefore the main creative force available to you. Indeed all creative work, whatever its form, is brought into manifestation in the physical and mental realms by some modulation of the sexual drive and the impact of the consciousness generated by it. In the act of writing a book or painting a picture, the underlying desire is often to have a deep and powerful connection with life itself of the kind that is implicit in every sexual act, even if in reality it often falls short of this ideal.

When it comes to sexuality most people are embarrassed to one degree or another concerning sexual intercourse itself. The sheer fact that they actually engage in such an activity is a problem for many people but they can not stop because the drive is too strong. Sexuality is an extraordinary gift. It is through sexuality that the life force of the soul is experienced and contacted most easily. The sex act itself generates large amounts of that quality of physical consciousness that shines through into the realm of the soul. Furthermore, it generates it in the exact location of the gateway from the physical to the soul body. Sexuality thereby provides one of the main feedback loops of consciousness between the physical universe and the universe of the soul.

The pelvis is also a place where soul consciousness is decoded. This is something you will all have experienced as having a 'gut feeling' and so sexuality offers you the chance to engage in a powerful dialogue with the one life energy, your own soul. It is also a powerful stimulus that helps to prevent you from losing contact with the fact that you have a physical body, a body that has its own particular needs. Many people are upset by the seemingly animal quality to sexual activity and the fact that it is so messy! Yet it is just such qualities that remind you that you are of the earth and the physical realm just as much as you are of mind and soul. To deny the reality and needs of your body damages your evolutionary potential in the same way as the denial of your soul.

Have you ever burned with desire? We have already defined soul consciousness as being like fire and so it has an innate resonance with all other manifestations of fiery forces in all of the different dimensions of existence. The sexual force, and its heat, is the most powerful level of physical energy that the soul uses to work with in the world. The physical sexual drive is in fact a perfect harmonic, in the physical realm, of soul consciousness—the consciousness that is love. In many cases the sexual drive, innate to all human beings, is the only energy that the soul can use to create change in a person's life. It uses it because it is such a powerful stimulus to action and relationship. Small wonder that so many have so much difficulty with it.

Few people have a true understanding of the real nature and purpose of human sexuality. Such an understanding can only come when the whole subject is viewed from the soul's own perspective. If we look at the process of incarnation from the point at which a new soul is created by divine consciousness, the first thing that happens is the need to have the right parents come together to create the appropriate physical form for the soul to take on and express itself through. This is not a waiting process wherein the new soul just floats around in its dimension of non-physical reality until random chance brings a suitable couple together. It is a period of dynamic activity for the soul in which, through its ability to contact other souls in its own dimension and their ability to manipulate sexuality in the physical realm, the right people are drawn together so that their sexual desire, which is activated by the impact of soul consciousness, can initiate the act that will create the new life that is so essential for the purpose of the new soul.

It so often happens that sexuality is the one thing that bridges both racial, cultural, age and class barriers between human beings. Some of history's greatest love stories have occurred because a soul was working to draw the right people together through sexual attraction. The problems, when and if they did occur in these situations, are based on a lack of understanding of the source of that attraction and its purpose. It is important to be aware that it can also be a soul's purpose to create sexual attraction between two people, not for the purpose of creating new life as such, but to allow for the completion of situations left unresolved in the past life of its companion spirit so that it can achieve a perfection of its being.

There is an enormous difference, or perhaps we should say that there can and should be an enormous difference, between the act of making love and of having sex. It is possible to make love at virtually any time of the day or night for any one of a number of reasons but it is not possible to have sex whenever your mind says that it wants it. That statement might seem strange to you but the sex we are talking about is true sex, not the neurotic pressured action of a man trying to prove his virility or make intimate contact in the only way he feels comfortable with, nor a woman's need to have her femininity and attractiveness validated, or one of the other variations that are so common. If motives like these are the basis of your sexuality then we must say that this constitutes a corruption of your sexual drive.

True sex is the natural culmination of the build up of certain physical energies and substances in the body and their discharge or transformation. It is rather like a car engine which, in the process of generating the motive force to move the car, produces two main by-products; the exhaust gases and a great deal of heat. Each of these by-products, one material and one energetic, must be eliminated otherwise the engine will either clog up or melt down.

The ongoing repair of the cellular structure of the physical body and the creation of motive force in the human body by the nervous system produces a particular quality of heat, not just physical heat from metabolic activity, but the fire of your sexual desire. We could also call it your sexual energy. The efficient running of the physical body requires its control and distribution just as the heat of the internal combustion engine must be controlled. This can only be fully achieved by sexual intercourse and total surrender to all the sensations that occur during the act and finally to the total release of the energy in sublime, uncontrolled orgasm.

The transmission of nervous impulses from your sense organs to your brain and from your brain to your muscles and organs in everyday life produces waste substances that must also be transformed before, they too, cause harm to your physical body. The sex act has just this kind of transformative power. The sheer volume of nerve transmission created during the sexual act literally burns up these substances and any excess heat and desire generated by the sexual act itself is also balanced out during the actual orgasm. This whole process must be repeated throughout your life if you are to function at an optimal level. It is certainly possible to exist without doing this, but 'exist' is the operative word.

Without sexual transformation the quality of life is so much less than it could or indeed should be. In fact, greater than any physical harm that might be done should this transformation not take place, is the corruption and distortion of the link between the physical and soul dimensions of your being. When you are overloaded with sexual desire, when your body is clogged with nerve function residue, the generation of that quality of consciousness that carries information from your physical body to your soul is seriously disrupted or totally blocked. When you are in this state your awareness cannot function properly. The reflections in your spirit are clouded. The gateway itself may also become so clogged that even should consciousness be generated, passage through the gateway would be impossible. Anything that interferes with your basic sexuality will make it impossible for you to live life to the full.

Most of the distortion of attitudes towards sexuality stem, on a world-wide basis, from the influence of the great religious traditions. Virtually all the major world religions tend to have a negative viewpoint on human sexuality because somewhere in the true uninhibited act of sex there is an experience of your own soul and the glory of God that does not occur through any earthly intermediary such as a priest, rabbi or whatever title an official representative of any particular religion might have. When Christ said, "The only way to God is through me," and "I am the way." He did not mean that he himself was the only way to God but that 'me' and 'I' are the way, in other words 'you,' 'yourself' are the way. The link is through your own being, not through some other earthly intermediary. In truth there would be no need for any kind of organised religion if everyone understood that such direct experience of the world of the soul is possible for all. The control and condemnation of sex, except for procreative purposes, is little more than a political move designed to maintain the various religions and their officials in positions of power and authority by denying you access to the one thing that will remind you that you have the potential for that soul contact within you already.

The act of making love is a celebration of the Earth and your own body. One of the major problems around sexuality is that people no longer have sex simply because they have the physical need. It has become a minefield of emotional and physical bargaining. For many women offering sexual intercourse is way of gaining the security of a home and of having someone to protect them in what can be a very dangerous and complex world. The men they partner can be said to be literally paying for having a sexual relationship by providing the required security. There are enormous numbers of men who in their own way bargain with sex too, quite often as a way of obtaining a mother substitute or housekeeper by offering the possibility of parenthood to women who deeply desire children. Sadly, it is also possible to abuse the sexual act in such a way that it prevents the kind of intimate dialogue with your own and another's soul which is one of the primary functions of human sexuality. In this case, something that is no more than a mechanical fuck or a shared act of solitary masturbation, is supposed to indicate a real intimacy between the people involved. Yet in this situation there is no sharing, no exploration, no love, no intimacy of being and definitely no soul contact and connection.

When sex is being used for either bargaining purposes or as a way of avoiding true intimacy the often expressed sentiment by the men who use it in this way when questioned about whether or not they genuinely love and care for their partner is to put it in very basic terms, "Of course I love you, I fuck you don't I?" When a woman uses sex as an avoidance their answer when questioned as to whether they love their partner is in effect, "Of course I do, I let you fuck me, don't I?" Men and women who abuse the sex act in this way are afraid of exploring their own true inner nature as human beings, let alone sharing anything of that understanding with another.

A true sex act, in a deep and loving relationship, absolutely requires you to experience your own fears and vulnerability. Such abuses of the real meaning and place of sexuality in your lives are rooted in the mind's misunderstanding of the true role of sexuality and its relationship to the soul.

Rather like love, sex often has great meaning ascribed to it by the mind when in fact sex and the sexual act itself has no intrinsic meaning. It has purpose and function, as we outlined earlier, but nothing beyond that. When you have some form of intimate encounter with another person it is often distorted by your mind. So often people ascribe some of the following meanings or variations thereof to sexual intimacy; that neither you nor your partner will engage in the same level of intimacy with anyone else, that you love them, that they love you, that you will get married, and so on. The reality is, that you can make your sex life mean what ever you want it to mean, any or all, of the aforementioned meanings and more. But remember, they are meanings that you decide upon. Your partner may feel that it means a totally different set of things. Just because your soul and that of another use sexual attraction to bring you together in order to do some particular work does not mean that your minds can cope. Your mental belief systems may well create a great deal of pain in spite of the appropriateness of your relating at a soul level. This is particularly true if there is little or no congruence between the three selves of the people in question.

Perhaps the greatest problems occur in relationships between someone who is well along the path of spiritual development and another who has not even begun, because their needs and understanding of the role of sex in their relationship are often so vastly different. It would be the mark of a wise person to ascertain exactly what your partner thinks having sexual contact means before you allow your relating to encompass this particular experience. It could well save you a great deal of pain later on. The ideal situation is when you both see sexuality in its true light, unencumbered by any personal demands for it to have any particular meaning. If you cannot achieve this position then make sure that you express very clearly to your partner exactly what it does mean to you and relate to them sexually from that degree of clarity. If they cannot accept or totally disagree with your ideas about the meaning of sex then do not have a sexual relationship with them, in spite of the prompting of your higher self or physical body.

When looking at sexuality we can see that any problems in the performance of the physical sexual act can have their root causes in either the mind and emotional attitudes or in the physical body itself. The basic physical problem with the sexual act is the inability to have an orgasm. This is a problem that is common to both men and women. It is commonly accepted that quite a high percentage of women cannot orgasm during sexual intercourse. What is less commonly understood is that the great percentage of men are also non-orgasmic. Do not make the mistake of confusing orgasm with ejaculation. Most men ejaculate, but few can allow their excitement to build to the level required for a fully transformative orgasm. In women the situation can often be the same as they frequently have an inability to allow the excitement to build properly. However, there is another problem that is far more common to women than men and that is that they can allow the excitement to build but they cannot allow it to release suddenly into a full orgasm. Before exploring the actual physical dynamics of the orgasm itself we will look first at the mental-emotional dynamics that can form a barrier to it happening.

For many of you reading this sex is, no doubt, a very goal orientated process. Your goal may be to be a 'good' lover, it may be to always have an orgasm or to always do your best to give your partner one. Whatever it is, it is going to create problems. Sex is not a competition. All goal orientated activity creates deep performance anxieties within the mind self. These anxieties are a powerful impediment to the natural functioning of the body due to the impact of the mental consciousness created and its affect on the physical body. Fundamentally, sex is a very selfish act, or it should be. Your concern should not be over your partners satisfaction when having sex. It should be focused on your own enjoyment of all the different sensations in your body. It should not even be focused on whether or not you orgasm, in spite of how beneficial that may be for you. Any expectation of, or seeking after, the orgasm will simply delay its occurrence. You must be fully involved in your own body. During the sex act your awareness must be very strongly active within your body-self.

It is perhaps true that your sexuality is best explored when you are young. When you are on the path of the self. It is hopefully a time when any selfishness you display, which if not fully accepted, is at least tolerated. It is a time before you have started to ascribe too much meaning to the sexual act. In reality, the selfishness we are describing is more at the level of self responsibility, of taking care of your own needs. It is not without consideration of your partner. If you are talking of making love rather than pure sex the situation is very different. In that case a totally unselfish concern over your partner, a powerful 'other' and even a goal orientation to show the depth of your feelings is most appropriate. Please remember that throughout this chapter we are only exploring the physical act of sex, not lovemaking. However, we must also point out that the very best sexual encounters occur in a deep and intimate loving relationship between two people, so please do not interpret what we have to say about sex as meaning that we are advocating a promiscuous lifestyle.

Another mental blockage to being able to orgasm comes from such emotions as shame and the related experience of disgust, disgust over the nature of the sex act, the proximity of the sexual organs to the excretory organs, and the memory of the many parental prohibitions such as, "don't do that it's dirty," often expressed to you in childhood to stop your natural sexual exploration. Many people also struggle with the seeming conflict between sexuality and spiritual development, the roots of which we looked at earlier. To develop spiritually you must involve your self fully in your body and sexuality. It is a vital part of your total being. You must involve to evolve! Your lack of involvement shows itself in many ways because the reality of sexual contact between most people is that it occurs between two uninhabited bodies. Rarely is the full awareness of each partner involved. Frequently, during sexual intercourse the greater part of awareness is somewhere in the mind not in the body where it should be. In this situation the mind is in all probability lost in self reflection and saying things like; "I hope this is going to be over soon," "That hurts," "This is boring," "I wonder if I put the cat out," "I hope they are enjoying this," "Do I look good?" "Did they orgasm or not?" "I don't like you doing that," "Oh no! don't stop now," "I am so tired," "I am not getting erect," "I am going numb," "Do I smell good?" And so on. We are sure you could remember many more.

Does it occur to you when you think of all those thoughts that you have perhaps had in the past, that somehow they might be indicative of a definite lack of involvement. A breakdown in communication between you and you partner. A loss of awareness and consciousness. Have you ever considered risking the intimacy of actually telling your lover what you think about sex in general, and all the various things you can do to and with each other in particular? Have you ever thought of telling your partner the kind of things you like them to do to you? Have you ever even asked yourself what you like and do not like? Did you know that everyone has a sexy soul? Do you realise that neither your soul nor God is going to condemn you for enjoying sex? What do you think you have a body for anyway! In the realm of the soul and pure life energy there is excitement, joining, merging and orgasm. If it is good enough for angels why not you? How about exploring your own body and sexuality to find out what you really like in terms of physical touch and stimulation? If you do, remember to share that knowledge with your partner. It could transform your sexual relationship.

Sexual arousal and orgasm is an involuntary act. It is, or should be, controlled fully by the body-self without any interference from the mind-self. The role of the mind in sexuality should end when the sexual act itself begins. As soon as penetration occurs the mind should let go. It has an extremely important role to play in all the events that lead up to the sexual act. It is the source of all the actions that are encompassed in the process of courtship or seduction. It is deeply involved in the foreplay that comes before intercourse through its appreciation of the texture, taste and smell of your partner's body. The true role of the mind is to act as the facilitator of the needs of the body and soul-selves. If you are a 'control' person, someone who needs to think they are in control of everything in their life, then you must be having some very real difficulties with your sex life. As sexuality is involuntary, any exercise of 'conscious' control cannot help but damage it. Active mental control is simply not refined enough a mechanism to be able to cope with the intricacies and subtleties of all the dynamic physical processes involved in the sexual act.

What is perhaps the major mental block to achieving orgasm is fear but fear of what? We pose that question because you may not be actively aware of any particular fear regarding sexuality within your mind-self. Normally, this fear exists outside of your ordinary sphere of mental awareness. The fear which we are speaking of, is fear of the amount of pleasure involved in sex. The sheer intensity of the excitement that builds in the body as a full involuntary orgasm approaches, is often terrifying to your ego. Firstly, any possibility of exerting control over the process is entirely absent. Secondly, the sheer volume and intensity of the physical consciousness that impacts the mental body is so great that it temporarily short circuits any activity in the mental body. Sometimes you may even feel that you are going to physically and mentally explode. When this happens there is a momentary loss of ego. This is to all intents and purposes experienced by the mind-self as a death and as all aspects of your being cling strongly to life the whole process of orgasm is often powerfully resisted by the mind. It will desperately send large quantities of mental consciousness to the physical body whose impact will be to make it tense up and inhibiting the orgasm to try and control its existence and ensure its own survival.

Apart from mental attitudes there are a number of physical impediments to being able to allow yourself to have the experience of a full orgasm. One of the major ones is poor quality breathing. Holding the breath is a way of decreasing excitation in the body. Decreasing the intake of oxygen and the expulsion of carbon dioxide leads to various changes in your blood chemistry and in the fundamental energy supply to the body. To have an orgasm you must breath deep, full breaths. Any partial breathing pattern will help to block your ability to orgasm. Holding the breath and partial breathing is always accompanied by varying degrees of muscular tension throughout your body. Active mental control of your breathing always involves you tensing up various parts of your musculature to maintain that particular pattern of breathing. The opposite is also true in that if you mentally hold different muscles in your body under tension then you will inhibit full breathing and concurrently the excitation required for an orgasm to occur.

Related to holding your muscles tight is the actual lack of any physical movement during the sex act. This is particularly true for women though less so for men as obviously the male is often doing a lot of pelvic thrusting in certain positions. Sexual intercourse is ideally an exuberant physical act that should involve a lot of movement. Movement that is fluid, relaxed and easy. Much of the pelvic movements performed by men during intercourse are tight and forceful because the muscles in and around their pelvis are in a chronic state of tension all the time. This tension drastically reduces the efficiency of the movement and the pleasure available during the sexual act. It is important to realise that pelvic tension is not just a male problem. Finally, lack of vocalisation during intercourse is another way of controlling excitation. We don't mean talking but moaning and groaning with sheer pleasure and excitement. Ordinary speech is an activity directly related to your mind-self, but spontaneous groaning is the voice of your body-self. You need to allow it full expression during sexual intercourse. We do of course accept that in certain circumstances there are good reasons to prevent it. However, if you always allow your situation to be a block to the vocalisation of your pleasure then ultimately you will forget how to allow it to happen. If you don't use it— you lose it.

The validity of all these points can easily be tested. If you have the ability to orgasm, simply try not to have one the next time you are having sexual intercourse. You will find that to stop it happening you tense certain muscles, stop any large movements and hold your breath. In fact, you may find as you feel out your body in this exercise and increase your awareness of the tension patterns in your body that you have already actually been decreasing the intensity of the pleasure available to you by always holding a certain amount of tension in your body all the time. You might discover places where you could let go a little more and increase the pleasure you already experience.

PELVIC RELEASE

To help release some of the physical tension you may have in your pelvis we would like to share the following exercises with you. First, a breathing exercise. Wearing some loose comfortable clothing including loose fitting underwear, lie down on the floor and place both hands side by side on your abdomen at about the level of your navel. Now simply breath deeply and easily for a few minutes making sure that with every breath your hands are lifted upwards because your abdomen is expanding and getting rounder as you breath in. Allow the abdomen to flatten and the hands to lower as you breath out. As you breath, be aware that you must not allow any muscular tension to appear in those parts of your body that are unrelated to the breathing process. Your legs, feet, arms, hands, and face should all be free of tension and as the focus in this exercise is abdominal breathing, the torso above the navel should also be relaxed. Once you feel you have mastered this, and by mastery we mean that your body stays relaxed and your hands rise and fall easily with every breath, place your hands lower on your abdomen, just above your pubic bone. Continue with the same deep easy breathing expanding your abdomen as you breath but now with your hands in this lower position see if you can lift them to almost the same height as your navel rises. In *other words making the whole of your abdomen very full and round as you breath in. Once again it is also very important to keep the rest of your body relaxed. Notice what happens to the amount of contact your spine and the back of your pelvis make with the floor as you do this. Continue with this for four or five minutes until you have mastered the movement. If you find this exercise at all tiring, or if you find yourself getting frustrated, **stop**. Please be gentle with your self, come back to it later or even tomorrow. You will improve with continued practice but not if you push yourself. The final part of the exercise is to try and push the hands up as your breath in but allow your navel area to stay low and relaxed. In this case the focus of the breath and the expansion of the belly is entirely in the lowest part of your abdomen. To begin with you may find it impossible to do this without a little tension and holding of your middle abdominal muscles but just use that to get a sense of the movement, then do it without any muscular tension in that area. As you do this, note the degree of contact the back of your pelvis and spine make with the floor and compare it with the contact made when doing the earlier parts of this exercise.*

It would be beneficial to do this exercise two or perhaps three times a week for about a month until all the movements are easy and you can maintain an overall bodily relaxation. After that it is something to explore every now and then, when the mood takes you, to see if anything changes and whether you can learn anything new from it. When you have finished the exercise roll slowly on to your side and stand up. Notice how you feel just standing then begin to walk about enjoying any new sensations you might be experiencing in your body.

Once you have fully mastered the above exercise there is a variation that you can do which is exactly the same except that you do not use your breathing to activate the movements of the abdomen. You use your mental control of the muscles of your pelvis and abdomen instead. Whilst lying down exploring this variation you just allow your breathing to flow at its own relaxed pace. Make the expansive movements of the abdomen just as outlined above by activating the necessary muscle groups but not in rhythm with, or using the help of, the breath, let the two processes be independent.

The second exercise is done standing and involves rocking or tilting the pelvis backwards and forwards. It mimics the thrusting movement of the sexual act. To do the movement stand with your feet parallel about hip width apart. Place your hands on either side of your pelvis near your hip joint. Move your body weight forwards so that you experience it as falling through the balls of your feet. Lift the front of your chest slightly so as to open up space for your lungs. Now breathing easily begin making very

145

small thrusting movements with your pelvis. Pull back your pelvis slowly which means that your buttocks will feel as though they are lifting back and upwards in an arc, thereby accentuating your lumbar curve, then slowly swing the pelvis down, forwards and then up, thereby flattening your lumbar curve, in a forward thrusting motion. Keep repeating this cycle of movement slowly and easily for at least three or four minutes feeling all the slight muscular adjustments as you move. Work towards making the movement as easy, relaxed and fluid as you possibly can. Make sure that you keep breathing easily all the time and avoid letting other muscle groups, not directly connected with the movement, tense up. Then begin to speed the movement up. How fast can you move without tensing up unduly and without the movement becoming jerky or uneven? Once you have found that limit just drop back from it slightly and continue the thrusting for another two or three minutes at this particular speed. At no time whilst doing this exercise should you feel any pain in your body, if you do then slow down and find the pace which does not create any discomfort.

At this point stop and rest, walk around a little if you need to. Now going back to the movement ask yourself which muscles you use to make the forwards and upwards thrust with the pelvis. The chances are that you will find that you are contracting your abdominal muscles to create the forward part of the movement. Is there any other way you could create the forward thrust without using the abdominal muscles? What happens if you draw back your pelvis just a small amount then relax your abdomen and push through your thigh muscles in some way. Experiment with that for a minute or two. Again draw your pelvis back just a little and notice what happens if, whilst keeping your abdomen relaxed, you just push against the floor with your feet. Does that move your pelvis forward? At this point you may have learned that there is more than one way to thrust with your pelvis. Now try making the thrusting motion, through a good range of movement, as fast as possible first by using your abdominal muscles then by using your feet and legs. Which is easier? Can you move faster and more fluidly using your legs to power the movement or using your abdominal muscles?

In terms of the sexual act, the less tension you have in your abdomen the better. Any tightness in the abdominal muscles restricts your breathing and blocks the flow of consciousness to your soul. You can practise this exercise or perhaps we should say 'sexercise' as often as you wish. Your focus is on making the pelvic thrust as loose and relaxed as possible. It is a powerful tool for freeing yourself up so that you can experience high quality sexuality. If it is available in your area you might also consider having tuition in belly dancing or Hawaiian Hula dancing. The benefits are similar and it can be a lot of fun doing these forms of exercises with friends in a group setting.

At this point it would perhaps be instructive to look at the basic pattern of excitation that occurs during sexual intercourse that culminates in what we call a full, transformative orgasm. The actual pattern of arousal during a sexual act that culminates in an orgasm resembles that shown in figure 15. It is rather like an

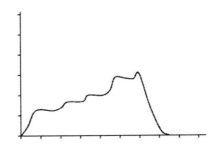

Figure 15

ascending series of steps that ultimately end in a sharp and sudden drop or release of the excitation that has built up. You could imagine it like climbing a flight of stairs with the occasional level area upon which you can rest before you move on upwards until you finally reach the top. With your last step you suddenly fall off, landing right back down to the level you began ascending from. The higher the line climbs on the chart against the vertical axis the greater the amount of excitation in the physical body. This excitation takes place over varying periods of time as shown by the position of the line in relation to the horizontal axis. The places where the line stops ascending are times when the physical excitation in the body is neither increasing nor decreasing. It is steady at a certain level. The sudden falling off of the line as it moves rapidly back down to a very low level of excitation in a very short period of time is the orgasm. An orgasm can only be said to take place when the excitation reaches a sufficient level such that a sudden drop in excitation to a zero or lower level state can take place. What distinguishes a 'full' orgasm from any other is that it can only be said to take place when the build up of excitation reaches the appropriate level but also that the whole process must take at least twenty five minutes from the point at which excitation began to when orgasm occurs. Without the sexual act lasting at least that long there is no transformation of the waste products left over from the neurological activity in the body. An orgasm can occur in a shorter time but no adequate transformation takes place.

The most common male problem with the sexual act can be shown graphically as in figure 16. This shows excitation rapidly rising reaching a peak and then suddenly falling away to nothing. The length of the process is much too short and the intensity is too low. That said, this pattern is normally enough to trigger an ejaculation, which is lucky from the point of view of the continuation of the species, but it is not an orgasm in any meaningful sense of the concept. Like the pattern of a full orgasm, this

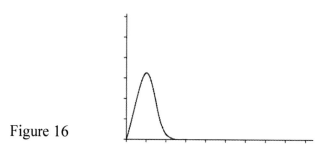

Figure 16

particular pattern is one of excitement and release and so there is a feeling of satisfaction in the experience but because the amount of excitation being discharged is simply not great enough to constitute a full orgasm there is no significant transformation or opening to the soul. The most common female problem is shown in figure 17. In this case the excitation takes place over a certain time period but there is a point at which the excitation reaches a maximum level beyond which it cannot rise and there is no sudden falling away of the excitement that has built up. Variations will occur in the amount of excitation from one sexual act to the other for the same woman but all experiences will be characterised by a gradual leaking away of the arousal

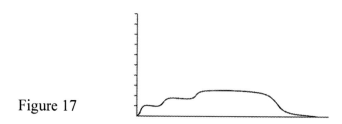

Figure 17

created, rather than any sudden decrease. It is a frustrating experience that leaves more waste products within the economy of the physical body than before the act took place.

Curiously the same patterns of excitation and discharge in a full orgasm takes place in another involuntary physical act, one that is generally less fun than sex and that is in the act of sneezing! Seriously, it's true. Sneezing is like an orgasm, not identical but similar enough for you to learn something from it about sexuality. The value in an exploration of sneezing lies in the fact that we are certain that all of you reading this book have the ability to sneeze, whereas you will not all have the ability to orgasm.

There are two types of sneezing. One which follows a pattern of excitation and release similar to that shown in figure 16. You literally just take one deep breath, as the charging up process and release it instantly in an explosive sneeze, "Atischoo!" The other kind involves three or four partial in breaths that finally add together to create a sufficient charge to release into a sneeze, the kind that go "Ah," "Ah," "Ah," "Ah," "Tischoo." This pattern of excitation and release is very similar to the full orgasm shown in figure 15. Each is most definitely a sneeze. The real difference between them being the time involved to reach a sufficient level of nervous excitation to trigger the sneeze reflex. How do you sneeze? Do you always sneeze explosively? Do you find it a satisfying experience? Do you always choke off your sneezes, so that they never really explode outward? Do you always furiously grab for a handkerchief or tissue in which to smother your sneeze? Are your sneezes incredibly noisy and volcanic all the time? Do you constrict them by holding your breath and tightening your nasal passages?

Having considered the way in which you sneeze does it have any relationship to the pattern of your orgasmic ability? For many of you there will be some interesting correlations. Have you ever had an urge to sneeze where the excitation built and built but never actually culminated in a release? Do you remember how frustrating that felt and how uncomfortable the experience was? If you have then you definitely have a felt sense of what it feels like to nearly achieve an orgasm and have the excitation slowly ebb away. You can hardly blame women who have this experience time and time again in their sex life for finally becoming disinterested in any kind of sexual activity. Men take note!

We can also look at another pattern in your life that may also tell you something about your sexuality and that is your normal pattern of eating. Do you like small carefully cooked portions or do you like large portions? How important is the quality of the food as compared to the quantity? Do you only eat at certain times of the day? Do you pick between meals? How many of your answers concerning appetite for food apply to your sexual appetite? There is a definite relationship between the way you deal with all your strong physical drives. Your sexuality can determine your eating habits and vice versa. How many of you men reading this come in and expect a meal to be ready on the table for you eat immediately as soon as you get home and expect sex to also be there available for you the moment that you require it. Conversely, are you the kind of woman who expects her man to be there on time for every meal that she prepares and for him to always be appreciative of it? Do you see how the rigidity of these attitudes and many others like them can be reflected in your sex lives with detrimental effects?

If you feel you have some particular mind level blockages to the natural expression of your sexuality may we suggest that you adapt the exercise on enfolding your body in love to help to resolve the problem or alternatively you could use the freeze frame technique to clarify and then alter the problem. To facilitate your orgasmic ability you have to loosen up in every sense of the word. Make sure that when you sneeze you do not hold on but just let it go and enjoy the experience. Break up your eating patterns. Eat at different times Don't have the supper ready on time. Serve a culinary disaster or go to bed instead! *Loosen up*! Do some gentle stretching 'sexercises.' Learn to move your pelvis. Try belly dancing with a partner! What do you mean we cannot be serious? Absolutely, sex should be Fun! There is a great transformative and health giving power to human sexuality but please don't pursue it incessantly for the more you reach for it the further it recedes from your grasp. Flow with the sexual needs of your physical body. Work on your sexuality for a time then give it up, regardless of your degree of success, and come back to it a few weeks or months later. Give yourself time to change.

Time enough to change. Time enough for love. Time enough for sex. Actually sex should take place in 'no time' at all. The experience needs to have a timeless quality. In essence, this means that you should not be thinking because the flow of thoughts and self reflections in your mental body determines your subjective experience of time. The more thoughts you have the quicker time flows. The slower that your thoughts arise the slower your perception of time. Do you remember how you experienced time as a child? It passed so slowly, precisely because you did not think as an adult thinks. As a child your thinking is rudimentary. Your mental body is taken up with the simple experience and absorbing information. There were no endless self reflections taking place. Have you noticed how the older you get the quicker time flows and just how much more you think, self reflect, cogitate and worry than when you were a child. An orgasm requires time to build, time and space in your mind, body and soul to experience the sexual act in its totality.

Are you always in a hurry? Do you move quickly and jerkily in short bursts? Do you think quickly? Are you fast on your mental feet? Do you find it difficult to change direction both physically and mentally? Can you alter a decision once you have made up your mind? Do you pride yourself on being a live wire, the life and soul of the party? If your answer to any of these questions is yes then we are certain that you experience some disturbance in your sexual functioning and in particular your orgasmic ability. Sexuality is a sensuous affair and for that to spill over into sexuality requires time, a languorous sensuous exploration of your own and your partners body, sensation slowly building and growing upon sensation until suddenly everything speeds up of its own accord with a dramatic shift in time and space and then a cataclysmic release. Once you have discovered this ability and you all have it, you will experience some truly extraordinary orgasms. In fact, once the ability is well rooted in your being you can experience a full orgasm very quickly, in a matter of minutes, which would not seem to fulfil the time requirement that we mentioned earlier. The reality is that the build up goes on long before the actual act of intercourse. Perhaps through the whole day—the original fourteen hour sex act!

Sexual desire in the physical universe functions towards the same ends as does the attraction of life energy in the universe of the soul. We could also say that if you understand the laws that govern sexual attraction then you also understand the laws that govern attraction at a soul level. One of the best ways to obtain this understanding is to explore your own sexuality. It is a unique way of coming to understand the creative process that is life. If you can deepen your perception of what is happening inside your own body when you experience sexual attraction for someone, or when you have some form of sexual activity, then you will begin to come to an understanding of the creative force as it manifests in your life and how it functions. The knowledge that you gain can be used in any situation where some form of creativity is required. We think you will agree, if you think about it, that even the smallest details of your everyday life would work out better if you lived creatively. Every tiny decision requires some level of thought and if your life is to be exciting and joyful, is should be lived creativity. The energetic and physical phenomena that occur in human sexuality are mirrored in the whole of your life and the way you live your life is mirrored in your sexual activity.

The other main function of sexuality is of course the creation of a new life but not every sexual act results in conception. Nevertheless every transformative sexual act creates something. If not a new life then new perspectives, inspiration, new thoughts and ideas, a renewal in your relationship with your partner. Sexuality provides a most powerful link between your mind and your soul. It facilitates the love light of your soul transforming and shining throughout your entire being.

CHAPTER 8

LOVE

We have already said that the power of love is power for the self, power for your own self transformation and the creation of your immortal spirit. But whilst it is power for the self it is not a selfish power. You may be wondering why if the power of love is power for the self that we have not spent more time teaching you techniques for creating the reality that you want. We have not because had we done so it would have simply pandered to your selfish egoic desires. The play of 'I want' within your personal mental realm and within your personality, are desires that are in themselves often totally isolated from the broader reality. There are a vast multitude of books on the market that tell you that you can have it all, but what they do not tell you is that if you get absolutely everything that you want it won't make you one iota happier than you are right now. You must understand that your state of happiness depends upon your inner integration not on you external circumstances. If you have ever purchased any of these particular kind of self help books we are certain that you have done so out of a perceived need to have more money, fame and worldly success. What you did not understand then, and perhaps still do not now, is that if you created these things and manifested them in your everyday life, your level of responsibility and worry would increase enormously. As soon as you create a structure, be it a new house or occupation, you are responsible for maintaining it in good repair. It is that constant pressure to maintain a structure that sucks the potential happiness out of the experience. If you want to build new edifices in your life then do so because you enjoy the process of building and maintaining structures not because you think that having them will in itself bring you happiness and contentment.

One of the keys in relation to the manifestation of your desires is to ask what effect you obtaining them will have on the rest of the world. You may think that they will have no effect on any lives except your own and that of anyone else very close to you like your immediate family. The reality is quite different. Every physical manifestation of a desire creates a structure, be it static or dynamic, that has a profound impact on its immediate environment. In some cases the effects will be fundamentally detrimental to some or all of the surrounding reality. You are a part of that environment, and if you cannot seem to manifest your desires does it occur to you that you could, in fact, be being protected by the subtle influence of your soul consciousness? It may also be that the soul consciousness of those around you, or perhaps of the planet itself, is inhibiting the creation of your desires because of the potential negative effect on their lives.

You might like to explore some of the desires that you have not been able to manifest from this viewpoint. If you wish to discover whether or not the manifestation of your desires will bring you happiness then create the desired conditions in your mind. Make it seem as real as you can then project that reality into the future. First a month, then a year, then ten years from now. How is it affecting your life? How important is it to your life? Do you still want it? Are you any happier than you are now? It is quite probable that you will sense yourself as being happier in the short term but in the long term we can guarantee that you will discover that you will inevitably want something else to make you happy. Then broaden your image of this new reality to include all the effects that you can imagine it might have upon the surrounding environment. Do this as honestly as you possibly can. Does it have a positive impact or not? Is there any way to modify what you want so that it definitely has a positive effect on not just your immediate world but upon all worlds.

As we mentioned earlier there are so many books and courses on everything from shamanism to positive thinking that say that you can have it all and that there are no limits, but this is a seductive lie that panders to the greed of an ego separated from its Source. The Earth that you live on is an enclosed, finite system. The spaceship Earth, as some have termed it. It does not have infinite resources, infinite space. Can you imagine if everyone on the Earth, all six billion of them, were to manifest a high paid occupation, a large house, an acre of land, an automobile (or two), a washing machine, dishwasher, drier, television, stereo system. If that seems too complex, you can just think of the things that you yourself want to manifest and multiply them by five billion. Where is it all going to come from? Could the Earth possibly sustain it all? What about the children, the generations to come, what if the Earth's population were ten billion? Do you still think that everyone can have it all? The people who really have it all are the people who run these courses and trainings because they are exploiting the unhappiness so many of you experience, and the false belief you have that more material possessions will make you happy. It is true that manifesting your desires will help—for a while, a week at least anyway. If you don't believe that the satisfaction could be that short lived just remember how you felt as a teenager when you were deeply involved in pursuing the path of the self. You manifested as many material things as you could in that short space of time. How long did the pleasure and satisfaction of a new acquisition last until you got fed up with it and decided that you wanted something else? If you think about it, in many ways the fundamental tenets of the manifestation aspects of these teachings can be summed up in a single word and that word is—Capitalism.

The whole Western world has been seduced for years by capitalist advertising and propaganda, which tells what you need to be happy. Advertising created by the manufacturers who need you to believe, for their own selfish reasons, that you can and should have it all. Always ask yourself what will the effect of having this particular product be on the environment, on the planetary being on which you live and depend on. Do not listen to people who say that your individual denial of a life based on rampant consumerism cannot help the Earth. These people are enmeshed in greed and a deep inner sense of futility and powerlessness. Their beliefs prevent the power of love from enlightening their existence. Truly any person's action can change a small part of the world, or at least their own immediate environment. When a hundred, a thousand, a million or more individuals join together, they can become an unstoppable force for change. Human life lived in harmony with the planet. Like the ripples created when a stone is dropped into a pool of water, how many people's lives do the ripples of your own reality reach and touch? How many people do you influence, one, two, three or more at any one time? What about over a period of five, ten or even twenty years? How many people could you influence through your inner integration and the way you express that in your everyday life?

Remember that you are asleep to your true needs. Such needs are often beyond the perception of the ego. They are rooted in your soul nature. The ideal would be to have a mind that never interfered with the passage of consciousness throughout your whole being. A mind that was a true reflection of your soul. With such a mentality you would always know your true needs. The creation of this kind of mind is a struggle that can, and should, be continued throughout your whole life. Be aware that there are always going to be times when you are more suggestible than others. Times when you could find yourself unwittingly adopting new mental beliefs that take you away from your body and soul. Beliefs that close the gateways between the different dimensions of your being. Appropriate manifestation is always rooted in an understanding of your soul nature. This understanding comes from feeling your way into discovering what is true for you and how that truth can be expressed in the world. From that will come the creation of some remarkable life enhancing structures for you to live within and take care of.

The outer circumstances of your life bear a definite relationship to your inner integration. You do not actually need to work with any specific techniques to manifest your dreams and desires. When you have good contact with your feelings your soul will automatically work to help you manifest positive experiences and material things according to your mind's desires provided they do not conflict with other people's or the planet's needs. It will enlist the help of the great company of soul beings to effect the required changes in the physical realm. A well integrated body, mind and soul will ultimately lead to the creation of your immortal spirit body. This spirit body creates within you, or is itself something which acts like a magnet, whose effect is to draw the most appropriate things into your life according to its understanding. They may not be the things which you think now or have thought in the past that you need or desire, but they will be the structures that are in harmony with needs of the omnipresent universal spirit. They will also be structures that you will be happy to live within and maintain. None of our comments on manifestation techniques should be construed as meaning that they do not work because they most obviously do. Everyone constantly manifests structures and experiences in their lives using techniques that are self taught or taken from various teachers and books all the time. However, in the short or even the long term many of the things that you expend your vitality on manifesting will either be unobtainable for reasons such as those we have outlined, or if your techniques are successful the structures will make you unhappy or fill you with stress. Be aware that an essential part of free will is the right to manifest things that make you unhappy.

In spite of what we said above concerning the existence of limits, it is true that there is one place where you can have it all and that is inside your mental reality. There is no limit to the changes you can make in your mind. You can change everything within your ego structure, all of your core beliefs and your emotions if you so wish. You can do so to serve the integration of your being and the creation of your immortal spirit or to feed the desires of your ego for a perceived better or happier life. Which do you choose? Strangely, you can also imagine that you have changed everything within your mind self without actually changing anything—now that is real power! Here there are no limits but the question remains. Does it have any effect upon outer reality in anyway? Does it affect other people's perceptions of you or do they think that you are just the same? It is so easy for your ego to fool itself and even the ego's of others. It can even influence physical reality for a while. Though more often than not, the ego simply refuses to perceive what is actually happening in that dimension, but just interprets events through a filter that allows it to only see support for its own beliefs and preconceptions. Indeed, if the ego is sufficiently rigid and isolated it may never perceive the lack of support for its position within the other dimensions of existence. However, no ego has ever deceived its own soul, or that of another. If you follow the path that is the Power of Love, you can be assured that reality will constantly show you who you really are, what is true and where you are deceiving yourself!

We have called this book the Power of Love, and up until now we have focused predominately upon its power to change your inner reality and your way of interacting within your personal relationships. At this stage, in the light of what we have just said, you may be wondering how you can appropriately manifest its power in outer reality. You may even be wondering what evidence there is that the Power of Love is being manifested in outer reality at all, particularly as only a cursory look through any newspaper will show you a world full of violence, pollution, greed and both natural as well as man made disasters. Just occasionally you will come across a story of some great or small triumph of humanity. A glimpse of the power of love in action. These glimpses come about when some person, or group, experience an opening, even if for only a brief moment, of all the gateways between their body, mind and soul. Remember the first time you fell in love, your first great love affair. Now there you experienced the Power of Love made manifest. Do you feel that you could have a love affair with life, your own spiritual development and that of the people around you? Could you extrapolate those feelings, experiences and perceptions into your life now? If you could, then how would that change it? In exactly what ways would it be different?

We suggest that you spend more than a little time exploring your answers to these questions. Enabling the Power of Love to act in the world can only come from individual action. You must manifest your soul consciousness in as many aspects of your daily life as possible. Ideally, you should manifest it throughout your whole life. It is difficult, in the complex world that mankind has created, to maintain an ideal position for any length of time but do not let that stop you trying with every fibre of your being.

The joy you experience when you express your soul nature and generate consciousness throughout your whole being—the song of the soul—has a power and intensity that can take it into the realms of paradox. Phrases such as, 'exquisitely painful,' or 'ecstatically sad,' spring to mind. Sometimes, the feeling of love moving through your being will be so powerful that it will feel as something is trying to tear you inside out. The intensity of the feeling can be savage and unremitting. Remember the Power of Love, the impact of soul consciousness is one of the fundamental formative forces in the universe. It is just as powerful in its own way as the most powerful sub-atomic forces known to modern science. It connects you to everything. You feel everything in both its pleasure and pain, its expansion and contraction. There is nothing easy in the experience. Like Christ you suffer for the world, exalting unto high Heaven, and all at once seeming to be hurled down into the depths of Hell. Once you have experienced this, you are forever lost to the ordinary world and enter the gates of Heaven to explore the real world.

The experience of the Power of Love is so often characterised in many modern spiritual teachings and literature, as being an experience of 'Love and Light.' That you are all 'beings of light.' This metaphor conjures up visions of beautiful ethereal beings existing in a perfect world and has nothing to do with the reality. Nothing to do with the power and passion of the soul and of life. Life which pulsates, scintillates, thunders, and roars. A Life that can also lie still, tranquil, floating or gently soaring, only to suddenly explode once more in a billion pieces of God. This path—the path of surrender—the path of power—the path of Love is not for the fainthearted. You must be prepared to suffer the agony and the ecstasy of the reality of your body, your feelings and your emotions. To be racked by, and with, the Power of Love.

The physical universe began with a bang. It will not end with a whimper. The same is true of your own personal universe, your own reality, particularly when it becomes one with the world of your soul. The experience of life and the Power of Love flowing through your body will often feel like something bubbling, welling and bursting upwards from the depths of your being. It comes from the bowels of the Earth, from the very core of your being, and the soul of the planet. It will sometimes feel as though it is tearing your heart out. It has to be that intense and forceful because mentally you all resist so much. It is the only way that your soul's exquisite consciousness, its love can emerge into, have impact upon, and thereby become part of the physical world. It is also the only way you can achieve immortality.

Teachings that advise you to live in the Light, or as they sometimes put it, that you should stay or abide in the Light are commonly interpreted by students to mean that you should avoid the dark. In particular, the darkness within your own mind, the demons of your personality, your ego. Often students of such teachings begin to avoid the outer darkness also. They begin to avoid and deny the pain of physical reality and

158

the suffering and struggle that can and does exist in that dimension. What they forget is that they as human beings must generate the Light and that if you generate the Light of Consciousness you are always in the Light even if you are in the midst of suffering and pain.

You generate consciousness by being aware of all of yourself and all of reality. By being aware of the dark side of your nature and in particular those aspects of your mental reality such as anger, hatred, jealousy, greed, vanity and pride. The aspects of yourself that you would disown must be a part of your awareness of yourself. If they are not, you will only generate an imperfect Light and the congruence of your three selves will be lost, preventing you from developing a character and later an Immortal Spirit Body. The angel Lucifer, the light bringer was sent to Earth not as a personal punishment, though we expect that sometimes he may perceive it so, but to help mankind to generate full consciousness of his whole being by acting as a constant reminder of the darker aspects of the human psyche. To help him and us to realise that it is only with that awareness of all of the aspects of self, both the good and the bad, that a more exalted state of being can be achieved. A being fully capable of creating such a powerful Light of Consciousness, allows it's brilliance to be perceived by the Divine, showing that spirit is, at least in one place, fully active. It also allows the Divine a very direct experience of the extraordinary intricacy of its creation.

The great principle that is Life itself has its balance in death. All movements in the universe have a beginning and an ending. The beginning is often referred to as creation and the ending as death. In reality creation is death and death, creation. These two flow in and out of each other ceaselessly. That which links creation with death is Life. The ability to bring forth your soul essence during your life, the period of your existence between the creation of your physical form and its death, ensures that the eternal process of creation through life to death to new creation continues. Your soul, which is not of the physical realm, is none the less tied to the life process of your physical form. It is important that the process that is your life does not come to, in soul terms, an untimely end. Should this happen the soul can no longer express itself in either the physical or mental realms. It is dispossessed. It cannot create another physical body nor an immortal spirit body. If it has already created a spirit body it cannot perfect it. The life process of the soul is ultimately terminated when the information concerning the loss of the physical and mental self finally passes back to Divine Consciousness, which occurs in no 'time' at all but which, in physical temporal terms, may be a minute or a year.

In ordinary human terms many people's lives are senselessly wasted through a premature death. In spiritual terms the loss is even greater. The possible creation of an Immortal Spirit Body is threatened by such an occurrence. A premature physical death heralds the total annihilation of a life process. It is also of the utmost importance to know that the growth potential of the soul, through the experience of life, is limitless. There is never a time in the life of the soul when it has 'had enough of life.' However, there is a time when the life of the physical body reaches a natural ending. A time at which it needs to release its constituent elements back to the Earth. Strangely, few people recognise this point even when they reach it, mainly through lack of bodily awareness. Indeed, a huge proportion of the human race never actually reach this natural ending to their lives. The time when their death blends into the creation of new and different life. Yet many people reach a stage in life when they talk of having had enough. They say that they cannot go on and it's all too painful. These words are the voice of the ego saying it has had enough of life. It says so when the reality of its inability to create the life it wants fills the whole of it's awareness. At this point, when the ego should be turning to God or its own soul, surrendering its will to the All That Is, it is driving a car in to a brick wall, slashing its wrists, taking a bottle of pills, becoming crazy, going senile, getting cancer or having a heart attack. It reaches out to embrace nothingness or a kind of living death if not actual physical destruction. What is embraced is not death. It has no creative possibilities in it. It is a return to the Void not to the Source of Life.

It has been said by various spiritual teachers that your death is always timely. That there are no mistakes. Yet the truth is that for most of you, your own death will be very untimely. Many of you who have studied with these teachers have no doubt come to accept their explanations concerning death such as: death occurs at predetermined time, death is a choice, you die at the right time, you die when you have completed your life purpose and so on. The reality is that none of these statements, nor many others concerning death are true. The truth is that death is not decreed by the soul or God at some predetermined time. It is based upon a natural completion of the life process, remembering that the life process itself is only natural when you are linked to your soul. Death should only come when the physical body has reached the end of its natural life. This can only occur with a body that is unhampered by any distortions of the mind-self and that has a clear connection with the soul-self.

It is part of your normal development as a human being to have the clearest natural contact with your soul when you are very young. Towards the end of your life, as your own death begins to loom upon the horizon of your thoughts, you naturally seek to re-establish this degree of clarity if you have not already done so before. However, it can happen through various external and internal influences that you lose that subtle soul link completely. This can happen at any time in your life right from your time of birth to the time of your death. If you have lost contact with your soul entirely, then the time and manner of your death is no longer related to Divine Consciousness and the end of your life could occur at any time and in a random meaningless fashion. In which case it could perhaps be said, as some spiritual teachers say, that you chose your own death. Though perhaps not the exact time, manner and place of its happenstance. It is a choice by default. Death should occur at a time and in a manner that is both natural and painless. A point that few people ever reach and that can only be recognised if you have developed the kind of profound self awareness that we have constantly advocated throughout this book. A natural death comes at the point when the body simply stops functioning and yet right up to that moment when the physical functioning ceases, the person will still be living fully and creatively. Loving and being loved.

As an example of what death is not like, you yourself may have known someone who said that they felt ready to die because they had done everything that they had wanted to do in life. Their life was complete, yet whose body was still vital, still powerfully alive. The reality of such examples is that the person's mind has become rigid and lost contact with the soul, so that mentally their creativity has been extinguished. However, the body, which is still in contact with the soul, still has great creative power. There is always power and joy in the experience of every sunset, every sunrise. Life on earth is so diverse, its potential so vast, that no one lifetime could possible exhaust all that it has to offer. Never say, "I have had enough." It cannot possibly be true. Even in the second world war, people in the most dreadful situations, in concentration camps, found beauty and meaning in a sunrise for instance. Never give up on life until your physical body demands it. Never go quickly into this dark place, this death.

Some spiritual teachers have said that 'ill' is an acronym for 'I lack love.' We could not agree more. All physical healing is nothing other than creating an expansion in the physical body, through the dynamic application of the consciousness that is Love. A Love that will then be transformed and flow on to heal the mind. Love is the power that heals, and any healer that recognises this is a true practitioner of spiritual healing. A total healer of body, mind, soul and spirit.

Physical illness itself is a fascinating subject. Most spiritual teachings say that you choose your own illness mainly through the process of negative manifestation. The meaning of this concept is that if you think negatively about your self and your body then you will ultimately reap the fruit of these thoughts by becoming ill. However, tell this to the person who is terminally ill with cancer or AIDS, particularly if they are in their teens or even younger, perhaps a mere infant. Tell them that they choose their illness, that they are choosing to die because of their negative thoughts! You might well expect a violent reaction or even a totally uncomprehending one, and they would be absolutely right to respond in that way. That negative thinking can create illness is true, but it is not the only cause of illness and it is rarely the cause of a terminal illness.

The whole concept of 'choice' implies a certain degree of mental awareness in that to choose something is a statement of a preference over a number of alternatives in any given area. To have a preference requires the ability to access information on all the various alternatives and then, on the basis of this information and any relevant beliefs that you hold, to then make your choice. When it comes to illness this simply does not happen because for most of you it is not possible to access information of any relevance on how that aspect of your being that controls your body, your body-self, functions and why any particular state of physical functioning or malfunctioning is occurring. Neither is it possible for most of you to access directly exactly how, for example, your liver functions. Of course you can read medical textbooks but this will not tell you how or why your liver is responding to any particular substances in your body in the way that it does. You do not have mental access to that kind of information. So to tell someone that they have chosen their illness is both a ludicrous and offensive proposition.

It is true that at a certain level of integration and spiritual development an illness can be a choice because at such exalted levels of development it is possible to access all the relevant information concerning the functioning of your body. The level of development we are referring to, is of course, the creation of your Immortal Spirit Body. To achieve this requires a commitment to developing an awareness of, and integration between, all the different dimensions of your being. A process that takes daily attention. Even should you achieve a full union with your self would you really want to have to deal with the minutiae of the healthy functioning of your body on the basis of choice all the time? Of course not. It is much better to leave that up to the part of your being that was created purely for the maintenance and repair of your physical form. Even should you have reached this level of development it is important to make sure that your mind-self does not interfere with the functioning of your body by dealing directly and immediately with any problems that occur within it rather than ignoring them. If you ignore the problems that can arise in your mind you create a situation whereby it may be forced to try and draw your attention to the problem through the medium of your physical body. It can do this by creating a disease that in some way symbolises the difficulty that it is experiencing. Ultimately, all that is really required to maintain a healthy body is to infuse it with the Power of Love then leave it alone. Your body-self will do the rest.

To tell someone who is seriously ill that they are choosing to be ill can be extremely destructive. It obviously means that if they accept that concept then they should be able to choose not to have it. Which would definitely be true if the illness was a mental choice in the first place. However, all really serious illness is caused at a very deep level. A level at which neither mental decisions nor negative thinking ever reaches. That there are thought forms within your mental world that are hidden from your everyday mental awareness and can have a definite impact upon your physical health is not in dispute. There are techniques for working with these forms such as hypnosis and appropriate kinds of positive thoughts and affirmations. However, these thought forms are not the cause of serious illness and so these particular mental body healing techniques are of limited value. Have you ever considered if it is possible that the soul might be involved in the occurrence of an illness, particularly a potentially terminal illness, like cancer? We have already said the higher self is a stranger to many people. For these people it is usually more difficult for them to discover their higher self's thoughts and needs than it is to explore the processes within their body-self, because at least they can accept the existence of a part of themselves outside of their everyday awareness that controls their body, namely their autonomic nervous system. How many accept the reality of the soul? How can you possibly find out about something that you do not believe even exists? Most, if not all, serious illnesses are caused by the corruption of the link between a person's soul and their physical and mental selves. When the link is broken love can no longer flow freely. Without contact between the three dimensions of your being, your soul cannot get its consciousness transformed and your spiritual evolution, the creation of your Immortal Spirit is blocked. In the end the spark that is your life will finally be totally annihilated at the death of your three selves. Nothing will survive, everything that is uniquely you will be lost.

A terminal illness is one of the few things that will force you and the people around you to look at your beliefs about Life, Death, God, and Love. It is often a final attempt upon the part of the universe—The All That Is—with the help of the soul, to wake a person up to the reality of their soul and the possibility of a part of them becoming truly immortal. It is however, important to remember that an early death never fulfils that requirement. The shock of being told that you have a terminal condition is often enough to create the beginning of a re-connection with your soul, but it could also create such fear in the mind-self that death looms closer than ever. A terminal illness is a devastating blow to the ego. It can engender a whole range of emotions from a sense of powerlessness to rage and anger. The overall life situation of a person who develops a terminal disease, such as cancer, is usually so hopeless from the point of view of spiritual development that the potential benefit more than outweighs the risks. The risk being the very real danger that the person does not make the connection and actually dies. Remember there is literally everything to be gained, nothing less than true Immortality.

If someone develops a terminal illness their higher self will then mobilise all available help to get their mind-self to the realisation that they do have a soul and that they do not have to die before they have created an Immortal Spirit Body. The extreme nature of this action can be too intense for a person to recover from. It is sad that so many people in these situations do actually come to an experience of the reality of their own soul and even create in germinal form an Immortal Spirit, but die anyway instead of continuing to love and explore life so as to give birth to and bring to maturity their own Immortal Spirit. To fully recover from a terminal illness so as to be able to walk once more into life on Earth requires nothing less than a miraculous healing.

A miracle cure for anyone happens when the links to the soul, the body and the mind are re-established. When the consciousness that is Love infuses the physical form once again, is integrated and passed on to the mind and back again. When this happens and the person recovers fully they are acting as the most exalted teacher to the people around them. They are sharing truly profound lessons concerning the nature of the Power of Love, Faith, and the healing capabilities of the human body. Even when full recovery does not occur, they are also acting as teachers only this time the lessons that they are teaching are different. They concern the nature of suffering and the ability to let go. In situations where you are faced with a life threatening illness you are being taken right to the edge of a precipice but you are never actually asked to jump off. The ability to turn around is a symbol of the reconnection with your own soul, the choosing of life over death. However, this is only the first part of the healing process. The walk back into life needs a deep loving soul contact from the people around you. The kind of love that does not demand a response but that coaxes faith like an open hand. A hand that is ready and willing to receive the hand of the sufferer. A hand that guides and steadies but does not pull. A hand infused with love that supports and sustains. When you have been that lost, the hand you need is the contact of someone else's soul. The literal physical touch of a soul that is still connected to the Light of the universe. The Light that is the Power of Love. It is that which gives you the confidence to allow yourself to move towards life. To once more take up the challenge. A loving touch that leads along the path away from the precipice. A touch that conveys that it is a beautiful world and invites you to come and play. This is a description of a total healing, a miracle, a healing of body, mind, and soul and spirit.

At that point on the road to recovery from a terminal illness when a person's link with their soul has been re-established, when the have turned around to face life again, they are at their most vulnerable. They are vulnerable to the needs of the relatives and friends who surround them. These needs are almost always a desperate desire that the person should not die so the relatives do not have to go through the grief and sense of loss that accompanies a loved one departing. All human beings have a natural resistance to being manipulated. The natural response to being pulled forwards is to resist by pulling backwards. When you are standing on a precipice the last thing you need are people trying to pull you forwards because as you naturally resist the pull you are just going to fall backwards off the ledge. Many people die just at the point when they could make a full recovery because no-one is there to hold out a hand of Love that is simply a support upon which they can stabilise themselves and feel safe for awhile, before allowing themselves to be eased gently back into life. The point just before a person takes their first step back to life is a critical point at which they must be carefully nurtured. At this point you must hold their being within your own *Love*, within your total being. If you are ever in the position of being with someone who is terminally ill and you want to try leading them back from the precipice you must work at sharing the truth and value of a life lived creatively with them through the example of your own life. It is valuable to share this vision of life with all the people that you meet because everyone is vulnerable at some time or another to doubts and fears concerning the nature of life, and it has long been known that very best way to teach is by example.

You may be wondering about accidents that result in death. In this case we say that they are never planned by any part of your being. They are always a mistake. They occur through a general lack of awareness. Sometimes simple accidents that are not life threatening are planned by the mind, in much the same way as it will influence your physical body to become ill. By this we mean as a way of attracting your attention to a particular problem it is experiencing. You could think of it as a cry for help. This can be a dangerous technique in that it is possible for the mind to be unclear about the real effects of an accident. It may be that what seems a simple way of making you aware of some difficulty turns into an accident with death as it's final outcome. Please be clear that this end result is a mistake, not something wilfully sought after by the mind. The best way to avoid all accidents is to become deeply and profoundly aware of your whole being and by working with all the exercises we have described throughout this book. In that way you can be sure of transcending the power of accidents.

In essence the whole of this book is about conceiving and giving birth to a personal Immortal Spirit. There is in fact another kind of spiritual child that can manifest as well. When we discussed the nature of the soul we said that the essence of the soul is Love and that your own higher self is the source of the only truly unconditional Love that you will ever experience in this life or ever need to. We have also spoken of the Power of Love as power for the self. Whilst this is completely true, it is only the first part of the story. An inner connection throughout your whole being is vital to ensure the immortality of your being, to give it the opportunity to move on through other dimensions of existence and fulfil it's ultimate destiny. Once you have achieved that internal unity and the creation of your Immortal Spirit Body, there is no greater joy on Earth than to join with others who have achieved a similar degree of integration. Should you be fortunate enough to have a male-female sexual relationship with someone at this level of development then you will perhaps become the parents of a 'spiritual child.' In fact even if the woman in this relationship bears no child herself such a child will be drawn in to physical incarnation somewhere in the world. In the latter case they will still be very much your child although not born of your flesh. This is the real meaning of Mary the mother of Jesus Christ having a 'virgin birth.' Jesus was not born of her and Joseph's flesh but was drawn in to incarnation through their spiritual development. The gift that Joseph and Mary received was the chance to raise their spiritual child, Jesus, in their own home as part of their earthly family. Jesus was actually brought to them to raise by the three wise men. Such spiritual children are a truly rare occurrence because not alone must the normal physical requirements of conception be met, such as the fertility of the couple in question, but both partners must have a fundamentally stable connection throughout their beings which must stay clear during the lovemaking and orgasm for conception to occur. Due to the difficulty in meeting all these requirements, the great majority of the few spiritual children who are drawn in to incarnation are not born to their true parents.

What is unique about a spiritual child is that when the Spark of Divine Consciousness manifests in the realm of pure life energy it creates a soul body at exactly the point before the life energy begins a new expansion contraction cycle so that the life energy in the soul pattern is not held in either a contracted or expanded state. What this means in effect is that the child has a soul that is both light and dark in nature. The spiritual child is therefore, it's own twinsoul, and soul mate. It is always fully aware of it's higher self and manifests its soul nature without distortion throughout all the dimensions of its being. It is a flame whose light is constantly shining back to its Source. It is born with all the requirements for the creation of an Immortal Spirit Body fully realised and so its Immortal Spirit self is usually fully formed very early in life.

There are other unusual events associated with the communion of fully integrated human beings. If we look beyond the possibilities that can manifest within a male-female union, to that of two people of the same sex or three or more such people, then we find that the 'spiritual child' that they manifest is not a new human being but perhaps a new perception of reality that has an innate durability that can influence human life for generations or even millennia. It could be a new religion. It could, in fact, take any form but what will characterise it above all is its durability and its positive impact upon the world.

The simple truth is that life is for living and for being creative. One of the fundamental truths about the nature of the Power of Love, one of the laws of Love, is that Love is creative. When we talk about being creative in your life we are not using the word just in the context of the creative arts such as painting, or writing. We are using it in a much broader context that means to live creatively. To live with Love as a guiding motivating force. Such a life may or may not include the exploration of creative art forms. However, it will always be 'soul-full.' Any creative act, which can be any act, any movement, is an action that comes from your soul nature. The simplest physical movement can be expressive of your soul. Life itself is but one act moving and flowing into another endlessly. When your every act is suffused with the Power of Love, with the radiance of your soul, then you can be said to be living creatively, moment to moment. However, do not get too addicted to being constantly creative because even as sleep and darkness is the balance to movement and light so too must creativity be balanced with periods of reflection and stillness. Awareness is the key to your creativity. Awareness of body. Awareness of mind. Awareness of soul. Develop and exercise your spirit to the full!

May we welcome you to life and immortality?

The Huna Training

This extraordinary boxed set of 30 hours of life changing in depth instruction in the ancient philosophy of Hawaiian huna is a must for any sincere student. The course consists of 18 audio cassettes in 3 library cases divided into 6 series.

Series 1. CONSCIOUSNESS
Series 2. SOUL MASTERY
Series 3. PHYSICAL MASTERY
Series 4. MENTAL MASTERY
Series 5. THE POWERS
Series 6. MAGIC

Designed to accompany this book it will deepen your knowledge of the Huna Mua teachings and all the myriad ways in which they can enhance your life.

To order the Huna Training tapes series as well the titles opposite please visit

http://www.masterworksinternational.com

MasterWorks International
"Committed to Artistry and Excellence"

MasterWorks International Titles

Available from all good book stores or direct from MasterWorks International.

A Promise Kept by Morag Campbell

An autobiographical account of a profound spiritual adventure set in England and ancient Kaua'i in the Hawaiian Islands. A companion volume to the Power of Love.

The Way of the Flamekeeper by David Kala Ka Lā

This book by Huna teacher David Kala Ka La offers guidance and suggestions to those who wish for more clarity about the steps that need to be taken in order to achieve self-realisation and know what it is to become fully Human—for only then can we become truly Immortal.

Quinta-Essentia by Morag Campbell

A study of the Five Elements of Ether, Air, Fire, Water and Earth.

The Art of Mental Wellbeing - The Polarity Of Mental Wellbeing and Mental Disorder beyond the Medical Approach
by Tony Caves

An exploration of sacred geometry and energy in relation to mental health.

Coming in 2005

Clearing the Soul Body Gateways - A video on this extraordinary and powerful approach to hands on healing filmed in Hawaii and the UK.

Printed in the United Kingdom
by Lightning Source UK Ltd.
123686UK00001B/154/A